THE DEADLIEST

HURRICANES THEN AND NOW

THE DEADLIEST

HURRICANES THEN AND NOW

BY
DEBORAH HOPKINSON

SCHOLASTIC
FOCUS

NEW YORK

Copyright © 2022 by Deborah Hopkinson

All rights reserved. Published by Scholastic Focus, an imprint of Scholastic Inc., *Publishers since 1920*. SCHOLASTIC, SCHOLASTIC FOCUS, and associated logos are trademarks and/or registered trademarks of Scholastic Inc.

The publisher does not have any control over and does not assume any responsibility for author or third-party websites or their content.

No part of this publication may be reproduced, stored in a retrieval system, or transmitted in any form or by any means, electronic, mechanical, photocopying, recording, or otherwise, without written permission of the publisher. For information regarding permission, write to Scholastic Inc., Attention: Permissions Department, 557 Broadway, New York, NY 10012.

Library of Congress Cataloging-in-Publication Data available

ISBN 978-1-338-36019-6

1 2021

Printed in the U.S.A.   23
First edition, January 2022

Book design by Abby Dening

Illustration, previous page: Galveston's awful calamity. This 1900 illustration depicts the horror of the hurricane that devastated Galveston, Texas, on September 8, 1900.

For Bonnie and Jamie in Texas
(and all the dogs)

Contents

PROLOGUE *Harry Runs for Home* xi

BEFORE YOU GO ON.......................... xv

PEOPLE IN THIS BOOK xix

Part One: Before 1

CHAPTER 1 *Path of Confusion* 3

CHAPTER 2 *Friday: A Change in Direction* 17

CHAPTER 3 *Saturday Morning*......................30

Part Two: During 39

CHAPTER 4 *The Cline Brothers: Like a Lighthouse
on a Rock* 41

CHAPTER 5 *The Kitten and the Baby*...............46

CHAPTER 6 *Harry to the Rescue*....................55

CHAPTER 7 *Voices from the Storm*..................63

CHAPTER 8 *The Cline Brothers: Drifting Out
to Sea*..80

Part Three: After 87

CHAPTER 9 *Voices of Survivors*......................89

CHAPTER 10 *Too Many Bodies* 112

EPILOGUE *Hurricanes: Yesterday, Today, and Tomorrow* 123

THE GREAT GALVESTON HURRICANE FACTS & FIGURES 137

More for Young Weather Scientists.. 139

GLOSSARY 141

TEST YOUR KNOWLEDGE *Fill in the Correct Words* 147

HURRICANE WORD UNSCRAMBLE 149

MORE HURRICANE ACTIVITIES 151

SAMPLE ORAL HISTORY QUESTIONS 153

TIMETABLE OF MAJOR U.S. HURRICANES 155

NOAA NATIONAL HURRICANE CENTER LIST OF THE COSTLIEST 159

EXPLORE MORE *Internet Resources and Lesson Plans* 161

SELECTED BIBLIOGRAPHY 163

SOURCE NOTES 167

PHOTO CREDITS 175

INDEX 177

ABOUT THE AUTHOR 183

Harry Maxson struggled through flooded streets in Galveston on September 8, 1900, much like this scene in Providence, Rhode Island, during a 1938 hurricane.

PROLOGUE
Harry Runs for Home

Galveston, Texas

Saturday, September 8, 1900

Four o'clock in the afternoon

The storm had burst by the time Harry Maxson started for home. Rain fell in torrents, slashing his skin. Gusts of wind beat against his face. He had twenty-two blocks to go.

Harry was just four-teen, but he was big for his age and strong. His father worked for the railroad and had helped

Harry Maxson

Harry land his first part-time job, hauling freight at the railroad yard for sixteen cents an hour. On Saturday, even as the storm grew worse, Harry and the grown men kept working until finally the boss said they could go.

By then, the water was already so deep that in some places Harry had to wade. But when he reached a street with only two inches of water, he began to run.

"I saw a roof being lifted off of a house. Believe me I sprinted as fast as I could as some shingles came toward me," said Harry. "I threw up my hand to guard my head and a nail in one of the shingles struck me and cut the back of my hand. At that minute—the wind, the water—dodging the shingles, I finally slipped and fell."

Harry's face hit the water and he licked his lips. Wait! What was this? He could taste salt. All this water? It wasn't from the torrential rain. No, this was the Gulf of Mexico itself surging over the city streets.

Harry struggled to his feet. The wind kept blowing. The water kept rising. His house was on M Street, close to the beach on the Gulf side. By the time he arrived around five o'clock, water in the yard was nearly a foot deep.

Saturday afternoon was just the beginning. The deadliest hurricane in American history had Galveston in its grip.

Not a soul was ready.

BEFORE YOU GO ON

This book tells the story of a terrible disaster, through the words of survivors. Their accounts help us understand what it was like to experience the Great Galveston hurricane. And that's possible because ordinary people took the time to share their stories in letters, oral histories, interviews, and journals.

Telling our stories is so important—even more than you might imagine. I wanted the accounts here to reflect various points of view and life experiences from both white and Black survivors. Yet, as I began my research, I mostly found accounts from white people. The voices of African Americans were missing. Luckily, I discovered a book entitled *Island of Color: Where Juneteenth Started* by Izola Collins (1929–2017). A Galveston teacher for many years, Ms. Collins was part of a family who had lived in Galveston for five generations. She was inspired to publish a history of African Americans in her city by seeing her grandfather Ralph Albert Scull (1860–1949) write in his own journal.

"I remember passing his bedroom late evenings, and seeing Papa (as we girls called him, since this is what my mother called her father) sitting at his little desk, writing in the green composition tablet," she recalled. He spent years recording his observations and experiences as an educator and pastor in the African American community.

Thanks to Ralph Albert Scull and Izola Collins, we can read the story of Annie Smizer McCullough, Izola's great-aunt, who was in her nineties when she shared her memories of the storm. We have insights and details that would otherwise be lost to historians, writers, and readers like you and me.

In addition to personal stories about the Galveston hurricane itself, throughout this book you'll find special sections with facts about weather science and hurricanes. And in the back, along with other resources, I've included instructions for doing an oral history interview with a relative or friend. I hope you'll be a history detective too!

We're all part of history. Your story matters. I hope you will tell it.

—Deborah Hopkinson

PEOPLE IN THIS BOOK

» *Clara Barton*

Clara Barton (1821–1912) founded the American Red Cross in 1881, following her heroic efforts to aid battlefield soldiers during the Civil War. She created awareness of the Galveston hurricane disaster and traveled to Galveston to help organize relief efforts.

» *Mary Louise Bristol (Hopkins)*

Mary Louise (1893–1987), who went by her middle name, Louise, was seven when the storm struck. Her father had died when she was a baby. Louise lived in Galveston with her mother, two older brothers, and older sister. Her mother took in boarders to make ends meet. When she grew up, Louise worked for the Santa Fe Railroad and married Oscar Hopkins.

She later visited schools to share her memories of the hurricane with young people. She died in 1987 at the age of ninety-four.

» *The Cline Brothers:*
Isaac and Joseph

The Cline brothers were two of seven children originally from Tennessee. Isaac (1861–1955) moved to Galveston in 1893 to head the weather station. He lived with his wife and three children in a house near the beach. Joseph (1870–1955) worked for his brother as a weather observer and lived with the family.

After the tragedy in Galveston, the brothers continued in the weather service. While in later years they did not keep in touch, they passed away almost within a week of each other. Isaac died in New Orleans on August 3, 1955, at age ninety-three. Joseph died in Dallas, on August 11, 1955, at the age of eighty-four.

» Milton Elford

Milton (1872–1930) was a young man living in Galveston with his parents, John and Fanny Elford, and his five-year-old nephew, Dwight. During the hurricane, they took shelter in a neighbor's house. He shared the terror of that night in a letter to his brothers.

» Harry Maxson

Harry I. Maxson (1885–1967) was fourteen in 1900. He lived in Galveston with his parents and younger sister. He had his first job, making sixteen cents an hour, at the railroad depot. His father worked for the railroad, and neighbors came to their house to wait out the hurricane. Harry's gripping account was discovered among his papers after his death.

» Annie Smizer McCullough

Izola Collins recorded an oral history interview with Annie, her great-aunt, in 1972. Born in 1878, Annie died on February 14, 1974, just before her ninety-sixth birthday. She was twenty-two when the storm struck.

» Thomas Monagan

Thomas worked for an insurance company in Dallas and was among the first people from the outside world to arrive in Galveston following the disaster.

» Ralph Albert Scull

Reverend Ralph Albert Scull (1860–1949) came to Galveston in 1865 at the age of five. A pastor and educator, he taught for more than fifty years in Galveston public schools, inspiring his daughter Viola and granddaughter Izola to follow in his footsteps. His papers, including *Black Galveston: A Personal View of Community History in Many Categories of Life*, are preserved in the Rosenberg Library in Galveston.

» *Katherine Vedder (Pauls)*

Katherine Vedder (1894–1975) lived with her parents and older brother. She wasn't quite six years old when the storm struck. She and her family survived. Katherine (sometimes spelled Katharine) married Peter Corlis Pauls in 1916 and stayed in Galveston.

» *Arnold R. Wolfram*

Arnold Wolfram (1858–1946) lived in Galveston with his wife and four children. As he made his way home during the hurricane, Arnold struggled to rescue a ten-year-old messenger boy who lived in his neighborhood.

This is a NOAA (National Oceanic and Atmospheric Administration) weather satellite image of Hurricane Maria over Puerto Rico on September 20, 2017. In 1900, weather forecasters could look up, but not down, on storms and clouds.

Part One
BEFORE

Galveston, Texas
Early September 1900

CHAPTER 1

Path of Confusion

"The hurricane which visited Galveston
Island on Saturday, September 9, 1900,
was no doubt one of the most important
meteorological events in the world's history."

—ISAAC M. CLINE,
GALVESTON
WEATHER BUREAU

Just twenty-four hours before Harry struggled home, the sun shone on Galveston, Texas. There were few signs a monster storm was on the way.

Katherine Vedder, almost six, lived in the city with her parents and her older brother and sister. Her father had heard rumors about bad weather approaching. Yet when Katherine looked out the window at five o'clock on Friday, she saw no sign of trouble. "It was a perfect late summer afternoon, the day clear blue and cloudless."

Isaac Monroe Cline, Galveston's chief weather observer, was also scanning the sky about that time. In fact, he'd been staring at the waves and the skies all week. He was hoping to make sense of the pattern, the way you look at pieces in a jigsaw puzzle and try to figure out where they fit.

But so far, the picture wasn't clear.

Isaac Cline was thirty-nine. He and his wife, Cora, had three children, with a new baby on the way. Isaac was a rising star in **meteorology**, the study of the atmosphere and weather. Since being appointed head of the Galveston weather station seven years earlier, he'd become a valued member of the community. Isaac had a lot in common with his adopted city. Both were ambitious and optimistic.

Today, just as in 1900, the city of Galveston sits on Galveston Island, a long finger of land, twenty-seven miles long and no more than three miles wide, that lies just off the coast of Texas. The brackish waters of Galveston Bay, an estuary, are to the north, and the Gulf of Mexico is to the south. Houston is about fifty miles inland; a railroad trestle across the bay was completed in 1860. (Today, a highway bridge connects Galveston with the Texas mainland.)

Founded in the 1800s, Galveston was a busy entry point for immigrants from Germany, Scotland, and Eastern Europe. Some called it the Ellis Island or New York City of the West. With its population of European immigrants, Latinos, and African Americans, Galveston was a multicultual port city. The city boasted a bustling waterfront. Trains brought cotton, wheat, and corn from inland farms to be shipped around the globe.

Grand mansions lined Broadway, Galveston's main thoroughfare. The city boasted a host of activities for residents and visitors alike. People flocked to restaurants, concert halls, and hotels, including the beautiful five-story brick Tremont Hotel. Surrounded by sparkling water and festooned with white oyster shells, Galveston was a glittering symbol of success, poised for the new century ahead.

Galveston's leaders had established a streetcar system and electricity services. They'd also built new houses. Isaac and Cora Cline lived in one of them, at 2511 Avenue Q, just three blocks north of the Gulf.

Not everyone lived in a new or sturdy home. As the population grew during the late 1800s, small structures sprang up on both the front streets and back alleys of the city. Some of these "alley houses" became rental housing for itinerant laborers who came to Galveston for short periods of time to work. Many became home to African American families and were built after the Civil War by Black carpenters, including Horace Scull, Ralph Albert Scull's father.

Hoping for new opportunities, Horace Scull had brought his family to Galveston in 1865, when Ralph was just five. In June of that year, a momentous event took place.

Major General Gordon Granger of the Union Army arrived in Galveston bringing official word to Texas that the Civil War was over and formerly enslaved people were free. President Abraham Lincoln's 1863 Emancipation Proclamation (which had freed any enslaved persons in Confederate states) had never been enforced in Texas.

Today, Juneteenth is celebrated on June 19 to commemorate emancipation. Juneteenth has been an official state holiday in Texas since 1980. In 2016, at the age of eighty-nine, activist Opal Lee, known as "Grandmother of Juneteenth," first walked from her home in Texas to Washington, DC, in an effort to get Juneteenth recognized as a national holiday. And on June 17, 2021, the ninety-four-year old Lee was able to celebrate. On that day, President Joe Biden signed legislation making Juneteenth a federal holiday.

In the decades after the Civil War ended in 1865, formerly enslaved people faced prejudice and huge obstacles when trying to get an education, a good job, or to own a home. Horace Scull worked building alley houses on leased ground, meaning the landowner usually rented out the house. In 1867, Horace built a house for his own family too. But he was forced to move the house twice because the landowner either changed his mind or refused to sell the land under it to Horace because he was Black.

The small, simply built structures available to Black families weren't as big or sturdy as the houses many white families were able to afford. These homes would not be able to withstand tremendously strong floods and winds like those of America's deadliest hurricane.

Around 1900, African Americans made up about one-fifth of the city's population of nearly 38,000. In addition to working in construction, some African Americans had jobs on the docks, thanks to Norris Wright Cuney, one of the most important Black leaders of his time. He served on the Galveston city council and helped create more job opportunities for African American workers on the waterfront. In 1889, he was appointed the United States Collector of Customs, making him the highest-ranking appointed Black federal official in the country.

Other African Americans began their own small businesses. Robert "Bob" McGuire ran a busy taxi service with a horse and buggy. He earned enough money to buy land near the shore, and built a bathhouse there that Black residents could use. He also served as a police officer.

The children of these early Black entrepreneurs went on to make a mark in their community. Horace Scull's son, Ralph, became a teacher. In the same way, Jessie McGuire Dent, daughter of Bob and Alberta McGuire, attended Howard University and then returned to Galveston to teach.

In 1943, while teaching in the Galveston schools, Jessie realized that Black teachers were paid less than whites. She fought and won a case in federal court to require equal pay for African American public school teachers. To honor this family's contributions to Galveston, educator and author Izola Collins became the driving force in establishing the McGuire-Dent Recreation Center in Galveston.

Before 1900, other Black-owned shops and businesses grew up in the area around Bob McGuire's bathhouse between Twenty-Seventh and Twenty-Ninth Streets. In segregated Galveston, Black families often didn't feel welcome elsewhere. Izola Collins wrote, "White owners of businesses on the sand did not want their patrons to be turned off by the presence of former slaves in the water with them. Such owners, and sometimes even police, told them to move on, that they were not allowed to swim in those areas."

Despite facing many obstacles, Galveston's African American community grew to include thriving churches as well as popular restaurants and clubs. Galveston's Central High was the first African American high school in Texas, founded in 1885. However, there were separate sections for Black residents in theaters, on the beaches, and on the trolleys. Galveston was still a segregated city.

HOW HURRICANES FORM

Hurricanes form over warm ocean waters in the tropics. The **tropics** are the regions of the Earth around the equator. These areas receive a lot of direct sunlight and are hot and wet, often with ocean temperatures of 80 degrees Fahrenheit or more.

Many times, hurricanes that affect the United States begin as a weather disturbance that scientists call a **tropical wave**, or an **easterly wave**. This is a special term for an area of clouds and thunderstorms that moves from east to west. If you hold your finger in front of your face and move it from right to left, this is how a tropical wave moves. (These waves are also known as **African easterly waves**. As you can see from the chart, hot winds blowing easterly from the Sahara Desert hitting the Atlantic Ocean help to create this weather pattern.)

How Do Hurricanes Form?

1 Hurricanes form in tropical regions where the ocean is at least 80 degrees Fahrenheit. These waters evaporate, creating warm, moist air—which acts as fuel for the storm.

The Tropics

Equator

80°F

2 Many hurricanes in the U.S. are caused by winds blowing across the Atlantic Ocean from Africa, which cause more water to evaporate into the atmosphere.

3 The warm, moist air rises high into the atmosphere where it begins to cool. Water vapor condenses back into liquid droplets and forms big, stormy anvil-shaped clouds.

1,000 Miles

10 Miles

4 As warm air rises, the winds begin blowing in a circle. The spiraling winds gather a cluster of clouds.

5 Once the spinning winds reach 74 miles per hour, the storm has officially become a hurricane. These storms can be 10 miles high and over 1000 miles across!

Thankfully, the GOES-R series of weather satellites take a scan of the U.S. every five minutes, keeping an eye on conditions that might cause a hurricane. This helps meteorologists deliver early warnings and keep people safe.

6 If a hurricane hits land, it runs out of warm, moist air and begins to slow down, but it can still cause lots of damage (especially from flooding).

SciJinks

Find out more about Earth's weather at scijinks.gov

A NOAA graphic shows how hurricanes form.
https://scijinks.gov/hurricane

As a tropical wave moves along, warm, moist air rises up from the ocean and is replaced by cooler air, which rushes in below. As it rises and cools, the water in the air forms clouds of water droplets, bringing rain and thunderstorms. The winds begin blowing in a circle in a counterclockwise direction. The cluster of clouds gets bigger and bigger.

This warm, moist air fuels the storm's engine. Because the air is moving up and away from the surface of the ocean, it causes an area of lower pressure below. The swirling storm keeps gathering heat and energy, spinning and growing around a center. Once its constant, or sustained, winds hit 74 mph (miles per hour), the storm is a **hurricane**.

In the center of a hurricane is an area of low air pressure, with clear skies and calm winds. It's called the **eye**. The eye is surrounded by the **eyewall**, with towering clouds and fierce winds. A clearly defined eye and eyewall are the mark of an especially intense storm.

A hurricane gets energy from the ocean's heat and

the water evaporating from the ocean's surface. That's why, once a storm hits cooler water farther north or goes over land, it begins to weaken and break apart.

Many hurricanes that hit the mainland United States travel up the Atlantic Coast. Some, like the Galveston hurricane of 1900, travel southwest of Florida into the Gulf of Mexico and may impact the Gulf Coast states of Florida, Alabama, Mississippi, Louisiana, and Texas.

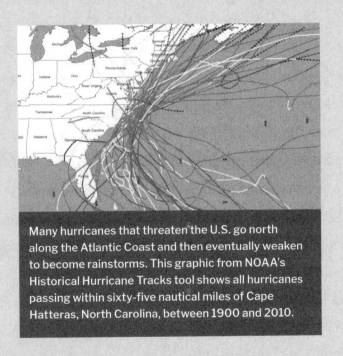

Many hurricanes that threaten the U.S. go north along the Atlantic Coast and then eventually weaken to become rainstorms. This graphic from NOAA's Historical Hurricane Tracks tool shows all hurricanes passing within sixty-five nautical miles of Cape Hatteras, North Carolina, between 1900 and 2010.

How Hurricanes Form

In the early 1800s, weather observers first proposed the notion of hurricanes as giant whirlwinds. In fact, these great churning wind circles can reach heights of ten or eleven feet. The word *hurricane* most likely comes from Spanish explorers in the Caribbean and Central America, who heard of a Mayan god of wind and storm called Hurácan or Jurakan.

In the United States, hurricane information and tracking is housed within **NOAA**, the National Oceanic and Atmospheric Administration, a federal agency dedicated to science, service, and stewardship. The National Weather Service, which includes the National Hurricane Center, is part of NOAA. Through these agencies, government scientists use sophisticated tools including aircraft, radar, satellites, and computers to predict and track hurricanes. NOAA's most advanced satellites are the **Geostationary Operational Environmental Satellite** (**GOES**)—R Series. To learn more about these amazing satellites and see pictures of Earth from above, visit: https://www.goes-r.gov.

A Hurricane Hunter in action.

Hurricane forecasting has come a long way since 1900. NOAA's "Hurricane Hunters" are specially designed aircraft that serve as "flying weather stations" and help forecasters and researchers make better predictions and learn more about dangerous storms.

In the photo, a NOAA P-3 aircraft flies in the eye of Hurricane Caroline. The circular hurricane eye is visible as a dark space in the clouds. This picture was taken on December 10, 2018.

Learn more at: https://www.omao.noaa.gov/learn /aircraft-operations/about/hurricane-hunters.

CHAPTER 2

Friday: A Change in Direction

Isaac Cline had set up his weather instruments on the roof of the E. S. Levy Building, located in the city's commercial district closer to the bay side of the island. He took his observation duties seriously. Ship captains and cotton merchants all knew Isaac and Joseph, his younger brother, who worked at the weather station and boarded in the Cline household. The dedicated Galveston team also included assistant weather observer John D. Blagdon.

Galveston was a deepwater port, which meant large cargo ships were able to dock there. This helped to make it a busy, profitable trade center. Because of that, the business community relied heavily on the station's storm forecasts. After all, there was a lot at stake: These ships carried valuable cargo across the Gulf of Mexico and beyond, to faraway places around the globe.

People in the area trusted Isaac. Just a few months earlier, his predictions of river flooding along the Texas coast had helped save lives. He certainly never wanted to let his city down. Yet in one way, he already had.

Galveston had improved its Gulf-facing waterfront. But even though Galveston was low and flat, in many places only five feet above sea level, the city had decided against spending money to build a thick concrete barrier along the shore, called a **seawall**. A seawall would help stop high waves from rushing in to cause flooding and damage to buildings.

Galveston's leaders must have felt more comfortable with their decision not to undertake this project when, in July of 1891, their chief weatherman weighed in on the need for a seawall. "It would be impossible," Isaac wrote in the local newspaper, "for any cyclone to create a storm wave which could materially injure the city."

Isaac couldn't have been more wrong.

Weather forecasters today rely on **weather satellites**,

radar, aircraft, and sophisticated equipment and computer models to track storms. Not so in 1900. Back then, observers in different spots relayed information by telegram to the main U.S. Weather Bureau office in Washington, DC. With roots dating back to 1870, the Weather Bureau was established within the U.S. Department of Agriculture in 1890. It became the National Weather Service in 1970, when it was placed within NOAA.

In 1895, Willis Moore was appointed chief of the U.S. Weather Bureau in Washington, DC. There, in the days leading up to September 8, 1900, Moore and his team were keeping their eyes on a developing tropical storm in the Caribbean.

For most of the first week of September, Isaac Cline had no reason to worry. The cables he got from the main weather office in Washington all seemed to tell the same story: This storm was headed north along the Atlantic Coast of the United States.

As far as Isaac could tell, this storm was not a

danger. It wasn't heading into the Gulf of Mexico. It wasn't a threat to Galveston, sitting just off the coast of Texas.

Except, of course, that it was. So why was Isaac getting such wrong information?

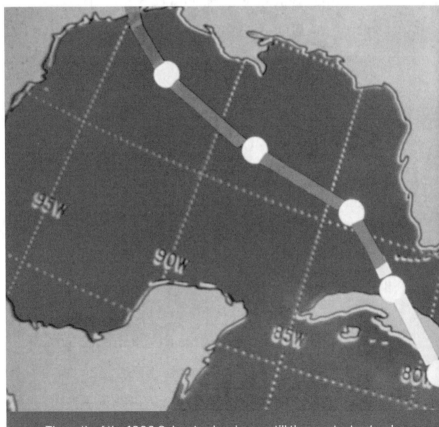

The path of the 1900 Galveston hurricane, still the greatest natural disaster in U.S. history to date based on loss of life.

The reason is a fascinating story all on its own. First, without sophisticated equipment, weather observers in 1900 relied mostly on rain gauges, cloud patterns, simple instruments to clock wind speed, and **barometers**, which measure air pressure. Since forecasters didn't

SEPT. 1–10, 1900

have a way to see storms from above, they relied on their skills and their experience of past storms. After taking readings, observers usually cabled their reports to the U.S. Weather Bureau in Washington via telegraph.

Humans did the observing; humans made the mistakes. In September of 1900, Weather Bureau chief Willis Moore and his team, including William Stockman, who ran the U.S. bureau in Havana, Cuba, made some assumptions and errors that had terrible consequences, ultimately costing thousands of lives.

The island of Cuba is in the northern Caribbean, only about a hundred miles from Florida, and had long been a colony of Spain. With the Spanish-American War in 1898, Cuba came under the control of the United States until 1902, when it became independent.

Both Willis Moore and William Stockman considered Cuba a backward place. They looked down on Cubans and didn't respect the Cuban weather observers. Moreover, they wanted to exert control. The United States was in charge now, and they expected the Cuban forecasters to fall in line. Moore and Stockman had even managed to ban Cuban forecasters from sending reports to other weather stations in the United States. Everything had to filter through Moore.

But Cuba boasted skilled hurricane forecasters, including meteorologist Julio Jover and a Jesuit priest named Father Lorenzo Gangoite, who directed the Belen Observatory in Havana. Father Gangoite had learned his trade from the legendary Father Benito Viñes (1837–1893), known as "the Hurricane Priest," who had built a network of weather stations across Cuba. This unsung hero was a pioneer in creating some of the hurricane warning systems used today. He was also famous for his ability to use clouds to predict hurricanes and his efforts to teach people about the weather.

The Cuban forecasters had been keeping watch on this particular storm system since the end of August. On Wednesday, when the storm passed just north of Cuba, Willis Moore and William Stockman assumed it would follow a more common pattern and keep heading northward up the Atlantic Coast. In fact, they expected it to be in New England by Friday. And they certainly weren't calling it a hurricane.

Meanwhile, the Cuban weather experts were drawing different conclusions. On Wednesday morning, September 5, Julio Jover published a report in a Havana newspaper daring to use the forbidden word: "'We are today near the center of the low pressure area of the hurricane.'"

Father Gangoite's observations of the skies Wednesday night and Thursday morning also convinced him the storm was growing stronger—and heading not north but west across the Gulf of Mexico, straight for Texas.

But because of the telegraph ban, he wasn't allowed to send a warning to weather stations in New Orleans— or to Isaac Cline in Galveston.

As longtime television weather forecaster Al Roker has written, "If Gangoite's predictions had been heard in the United States, there would have been time to give the people of Galveston and the Texas mainland a fairly long-range warning of the impending destruction."

While throughout that week, Isaac had no reason to believe a storm was on its way, on Friday morning, September 7, he received a surprising update.

The U.S. Weather Bureau was now reporting that the tropical storm wasn't heading north up the Atlantic Coast after all. Willis Moore had gotten no reports of wind or strong rains from states on the Atlantic Coast. What had happened to the storm?

Willis Moore had to conclude that since leaving Cuba on Wednesday, the storm had veered westerly and was somewhere in the Gulf of Mexico—just as Father Gangoite had predicted. So on Friday, Moore gave Isaac orders to hoist a red-and-black storm warning flag. Moore had to accept the Cuban forecasters' conclusion about the storm's direction.

However, since most hurricanes didn't travel in this pattern, Moore still didn't believe the Cubans were correct about the storm's severity. He didn't believe that it was a hurricane. He thought it was a heavy storm with high winds, no more than that. And so the word *hurricane* wasn't mentioned in the storm warning Moore sent to Isaac.

Heavy rains were common in early September, so Isaac wasn't terribly alarmed. Besides, he later wrote, "The usual signs which herald the approach of hurricanes were not present in this case. The brick-dust sky was not in evidence to the smallest degree."

When Isaac hoisted the storm warning flag on Friday, the sky was mostly a clear bright blue.

HURRICANE, CYCLONE, OR TYPHOON?

There are several different words used in various parts of the world to describe deadly storms.

Tropical cyclone is the general term meteorologists use for storms that begin in warm tropical oceans and have strong circulating winds that rotate around a center of low pressure. This term is also used for severe storms of hurricane force (winds more than 74 mph) when they occur in the South Pacific and Indian Oceans.

A severe tropical cyclone with constant wind speeds of 74 mph or more is called a **typhoon** or hurricane, depending on where it occurs. In the North Atlantic and northeast Pacific Ocean east of the International Date Line (IDL), and the South Pacific Ocean east of 160 degrees, it's called a hurricane. It's called a typhoon if it occurs in the northwest Pacific Ocean west of the International Date Line.

One thing is different within the storm itself, depending on where it occurs. North of the equator, in the Northern Hemisphere, the winds rotate

Artist's rendition of the eye of a hurricane.

in a counterclockwise direction. In the Southern Hemisphere, winds rotate clockwise. This difference is due to Earth's rotation on its axis.

What about storms that are less severe? Scientists use special terms to distinguish storms of lower intensity. A tropical cyclone with maximum sustained surface winds of at least 39 mph but less than 74 mph is called a **tropical storm**. If the winds are less than 39 mph, we call it a **tropical depression**. Weather forecasters watch these areas carefully to see if they will develop into more ferocious storms.

CHAPTER 3
Saturday Morning

J oseph Cline, like Isaac, was fascinated by weather. The brothers had grown up on a farm in Tennessee, part of a large family of four boys and three girls.

Joseph and Isaac were hardworking, smart, and ambitious. "On the dark, cold winter mornings, my brothers and I would start the day early by eating breakfast, feeding the livestock, and being off to the fields by daylight," Joseph remembered.

Isaac had gone to medical school. Joseph had been a teacher and worked for the railroad before accepting his brother's offer to become an assistant weather observer. Joseph was determined to do well and learned all he could about weather science. "I applied myself to my new job with all the diligence at my command. I studied night and day, absorbing all the current text-book material on meteorology."

Even before he woke up on Saturday, Joseph had a premonition something was wrong. Sure enough, he discovered water in their yard washing in from the Gulf beach a few blocks away. He woke Isaac and the brothers conferred. Isaac decided to investigate.

Although they were close enough to walk to the beach, Isaac wanted to cover as much ground as possible. So he hitched up his horse and wagon and drove along the shoreline, timing and measuring the swells. A wave forms when wind blows over the surface of the water. A **swell** is the term for a series of waves. These waves have formed farther away and traveled across the water. Stronger-than-usual swells are a signal that a storm system with high winds is approaching.

Isaac watched carefully for swells gaining in size and frequency. And that's exactly what he saw. The swells were rolling in about one to five minutes apart, and growing larger all the time. That worried Isaac, because even though the wind was blowing from the shore *against* the waves, they kept getting bigger. The swells were pushing seawater farther and farther up the beach. That explained the water in their yard.

Isaac sent a telegram to the Weather Bureau office in Washington, DC, to report what he was observing: "Unusually heavy swells from the southeast, intervals

An example of a storm surge. This photo depicts sixteen feet of storm surge striking the Florida Panhandle during Hurricane Eloise in September of 1975. In coastal communities, higher-than-usual swells and the rising sea level caused by an approaching storm can wreak considerable damage. Large waves are fascinating but dangerous.

one to five minutes, overflowing low places south portion of city three to four blocks from beach. Such high water with opposing winds never observed previously."

Even then, Isaac still underestimated the strength of the approaching storm. He expected flooding and warned some shopkeepers and merchants. He suggested they move their goods at least three feet off the floor. That would not be nearly enough.

And while Isaac warned some people, since only the main U.S. Weather Bureau in Washington could issue hurricane warnings, the weather report in Saturday's *Galveston News* didn't alarm anyone. Buried on page ten was this note: "'The weather bureau officials did not anticipate any dangerous disturbance.'"

Families in Galveston had no reason to prepare or panic. They simply went about their usual Saturday routines. Later, a young woman named Sarah Hawley wrote her mother, "Friday evening the wind was very strong and Saturday morning it was even stronger, the sky dark, but otherwise there was nothing unusual."

Nothing unusual.

That changed as the day went on and weather conditions worsened by the hour. The wind picked up. It began to rain. Isaac and Joseph kept up their observations. Isaac patrolled the beach, urging people to take shelter. By three thirty on Saturday afternoon, the wind had become ferocious; the waves grew into monsters. Water poured onto the city streets.

Isaac asked Joseph to send a telegram to Washington: "Gulf rising, water covers streets of about half the city."

Wading through knee-deep water, Joseph reached the Western Union office. He was told the wires were down and nothing could go out. He tried another telegraph office with the same result. Joseph returned to his office and was finally able to make a long-distance call and get the report through. It would be the last message from Galveston before the disaster.

Joseph left the office and made a sweep of the beach area, trying to warn as many people as he could to move inland. Then he headed to Isaac's house. John Blagdon, another assistant, stayed in the office to monitor the weather instruments, especially the barometer. The rain gauge on the roof blew away around six o'clock on Saturday night, but Blagdon bravely stayed at his post and continued to take barometer readings.

At five o'clock, the barometer read 29.05. At ten past eight, it had dropped to 28.53. These readings, Isaac later noted, "indicate the great intensity of the hurricane."

WHAT DOES A BAROMETER MEASURE?

Earth's atmosphere has weight and pushes down on anything below. Weather forecasters can measure this **air pressure**, or **atmospheric pressure**, using an instrument called a barometer.

Back in the 1600s, the noted Italian astronomer Galileo Galilei performed early experiments to show that although it is invisible, air has weight. In 1646, an Italian scientist named Evangelista Torricelli designed an instrument, later called a *barometer*, to measure air pressure using a glass tube and mercury. (The word *barometer* comes from the Greek *baros*, meaning "weight.")

By 1900, weather forecasters routinely used barometers and knew that high pressure signaled fair weather and falling barometric pressure heralded bad weather. Remember, in hurricanes, warm, moist air rises up from the surface of the ocean. As the winds lift the air, the warm air rises higher. There is less air near the surface, making this an area of lower air pressure.

The normal air pressure at sea level is 29.92126 inches. According to Guinness World Records, the lowest air pressure ever recorded was 25.69 inches in 1979 about three hundred miles west of Guam in the eye of Typhoon Tip.

NOAA photograph of the eyewall of a hurricane taken by aircraft.

Part Two
DURING

Saturday Afternoon–Sunday Dawn

"The wreck of Galveston was brought
about by a tempest so terrible that
no words can adequately describe its
intensity, and by a flood which turned
the city into a raging sea."

—RICHARD SPILLANE,
NEW YORK TIMES,
SEPTEMBER 11, 1900

CHAPTER 4

The Cline Brothers:
Like a Lighthouse on a Rock

On Saturday afternoon, Joseph Cline had barely managed to send Galveston's last message to the outside world. After that, he walked up and down for a mile on the beach, warning everyone he saw. When he arrived at Isaac's house in the early evening, the family and neighbors had already gathered.

At first, Joseph thought they'd be safe there, although they were very close to the beach. Surely, Isaac's two-story house, built only four years before, could take a beating. The house, Joseph later wrote, was "like a lighthouse built upon a rock."

Meanwhile, Isaac continued to make weather observations from his doorstep; he invited more neighbors in from smaller houses nearby. About fifty frightened people crowded inside.

As day turned to evening and the wind and rain grew fiercer, Joseph began to wonder if even this sturdy structure could stand. He called Isaac outside to discuss his fears. Joseph thought they should make an attempt to move toward the center of town, on the other side of the island.

"At this time, however, the roofs of houses and timbers were flying through the streets as though they were paper," Isaac wrote later. Isaac believed it would be too dangerous to move, especially since Cora, his wife, was unwell.

As the brothers stood talking, they witnessed the **storm surge**: an abnormal rise in sea level from an intense storm or hurricane. Isaac and Joseph could only watch, helpless, as the water was pushed onto shore, powered by the hurricane's fierce winds as it hit land after traveling hundreds of miles unimpeded across the Gulf of Mexico.

Isaac later reported, "The water rose at a steady rate from 3 p.m. until about 7:30 p.m., when there was a sudden rise of about four feet in as many seconds. I was standing at my front door, which was partly open, watching the water which was flowing with great rapidity from east to west. The water at this time was about eight inches deep in my residence, and the sudden rise of 4 feet brought it above my waist before I could change my position.

"The water had now reached a stage 10 feet above the ground at Rosenberg Avenue (Twenty-fifth Street) and Q Street, where my residence stood. The ground was 5.2 feet elevation, which made the tide 15.2 feet. The tide rose the next hour, between 7:30 and 8:30 p.m., nearly five feet additional, making a total tide in that locality of about twenty feet."

Isaac and Joseph rushed back inside and herded everyone upstairs. Before dark, the house stood in fifteen feet of water.

Their chance of escape was gone.

DANGEROUS STORM SURGES

According to NOAA, the storm surge of a hurricane poses the greatest threat to people and property along the coast.

When combined with the normal tides of the sea, a storm surge often increases the water level by fifteen feet or even more. This can cause severe flooding and damage, especially in places where the coastline is not far above sea level and there are many buildings and houses near the beach. Nowadays, the National Weather Service will issue storm surge warnings so people can be prepared for these life-threatening events.

But there was no warning back in 1900, when the hurricane struck Galveston straight on, creating a devastating storm surge of at least fifteen feet or higher in some places. This brought massive destruction and flooding along with high winds, which experts estimate may have reached 140 mph.

This U.S. Navy photo illustrates how storm surges push water ashore, posing a danger to structures on land. In the same way, the storm surge of the Galveston hurricane threatened Isaac Cline's house.

CHAPTER 5
The Kitten and the Baby

Katherine Vedder's house was about half a mile from the Gulf beach and two miles west of Isaac Cline's house. Late Saturday morning, her older brother, Jacob, and her cousin Allen began racing back and forth to the beach to look at the big waves crashing in.

At first, it seemed exciting—until the boys returned with frightening news. "About half past three, Jacob and Allen came running, shouting excitedly that the Gulf looked like a great gray wall about fifty feet high and moving slowly toward the island," Katherine said.

Katherine's father worried their house wouldn't survive. He told his family that if the house began to break apart, they should tie themselves together and try to make their way to the home of their neighbor, Richard

This historic photo shows storm damage on the New Jersey shore around 1914. As global climate change makes oceans warmer, coastal areas worldwide face severe threats. In Galveston, Katherine Vedder and her family lived about a half mile from the beach. Most of the homes near theirs were totally destroyed.

Peek. He believed the Peeks' house could withstand any storm. For now, though, the Vedder family would stay put.

It turned out to be the wisest decision they made.

As fierce winds rattled the windows, neighbors who lived in small cottages and alley houses drifted in to join the Vedder family. Some soldiers from nearby Fort Crockett arrived too.

Peopled huddled on the stairs to the second floor. Katherine's father took down two inside doors and nailed them crosswise to reinforce the front door. Katherine and friends, Francesca Mason and her brother, Kearny, played with Katherine's kitten. Before it grew dark, Katherine could see the water outside covering four-foot fences. Water was seeping into the house by now, slowly rising. Everyone hoped the next gust of wind wouldn't blow off the roof.

Suddenly, Katherine felt a tremendous jolt. Next came a strange sensation, like a boat going over a big wave. Only they weren't supposed to be in a boat, they were supposed to be on land! Except they weren't. Katherine said, "The house rose, floated from its six-foot foundation and with a terrific jolt, settled on the ground."

Without its sturdy foundation, the house was now

sitting dangerously lower in the flood. Inside, the water level instantly rose about five feet, covering the children completely. The soldiers groped frantically and managed to fish all three out. The soldiers then "handed us, gasping and dripping, to our mothers, who had fled higher up the stairs," Katherine remembered.

But what about the kitten? All at once, Katherine spied it. "I called out, 'Papa, there's my kitten.' He pulled a soaking, clawing bit of fur from the water and tossed it up the stairs.

"Mrs. Mason caught it and shrieking, 'It's a rat,' tossed it back into the water. It was sometime before the kitten was safe in my arms."

The tiny kitten survived. It would have a vital role to play that night.

The family's house had been torn from its foundation, but it was still standing. A long and frightening night stretched before everyone inside. The wind ripped away the roof from over two upstairs bedrooms, so people crowded into a bathroom that still offered

Although the Vedder family home survived the hurricane, thousands of others in Galveston were destroyed.

protection from the pouring rain. Katherine's mother wrapped Katherine and her friend Francesca in a bed-spread and put the girls into the tub for safety.

Downstairs, Katherine's father realized the struggle had just begun. Their house was near the new barracks at Fort Crockett, which had been constructed of large beams, twelve inches around and twenty feet long. Some of those very beams were now floating through the floodwaters, acting like massive battering rams.

Katherine's father was especially worried about the

front door, the weakest part of the house. When the house settled, a hole had opened near the front door but above water level. With his bare arms, Katherine's father reached through. Time and again, he pushed away the beams floating dangerously close.

His quick thinking saved the house. "But for months after he suffered agony as the doctor probed and worked over his torn and lacerated arms and hands, for they were filled with glass, splinters, and other foreign matter which swept by on the waters of the storm," Katherine said. Her father carried scars on his hands the rest of his life.

Katherine's kitten was not the only little one rescued that night. Another cry for help came in the early morning hours. A couple was spotted staggering along through the muddy, churning waters, carrying their lifeless six-week-old baby. Their house was gone and now they fought their way through the flood to try to reach a safe place.

When they were pulled inside, it seemed as though

the tiny baby was dead. But Katherine's mother wasn't about to give up.

"My mother took him and saw that there was still a spark of life," Katherine recalled. "She crawled on her hands and knees through the darkness into the northeast room where, from an overturned bureau and cabinet, she pulled a knitted woolen petticoat and a broken bottle of blackberry cordial.

"Making her way back in the pitch black dark she stripped the baby of its wet clothing and wrapped it in the woolen garment and placed the now dry and purring kitten next to the baby's body for warmth."

Then the baby's mom took some of the sweet, slightly alcoholic drink into her mouth and transferred it, drop by drop, to her baby's mouth, making sure no glass from the broken bottle passed through her lips.

Katherine said, "Gradually the tiny cold body grew warm and soon a wailing infant demanded food."

One tiny kitten had helped save a baby.

GET TRACKING!

The Galveston hurricane struck in early September, during peak **hurricane season** in the North Atlantic. The season runs from the first of June through November 30.

While people in Galveston couldn't track the storm, today's citizen scientists can visit NOAA's National Hurricane Center, which includes a page where you can track big storms across the globe: https://www.nhc.noaa.gov.

You can also download a blank tracking map: https://www.nhc.noaa.gov/AT_Track_chart.pdf.

A **hurricane watch** puts people on alert. When a tropical storm draws closer, a **hurricane warning** is issued, sometimes days in advance. There's a good reason for the advance warning: It takes time to evacuate large cities or coastal areas.

The Deadliest Hurricanes Then and Now

Historically, 97 percent of intense storms have occurred within these June through November dates. That's because conditions then are the most likely to create large storms.

However, there's nothing magical about those dates. According to NOAA, "All it takes is the right combination of atmospheric conditions and warmer ocean waters for a tropical cyclone to form, regardless of the date."

CHAPTER 6
Harry to the Rescue

When fourteen-year-old Harry Maxson made it home late Saturday afternoon, his mother and younger brother and sister were anxiously waiting for him. Harry's father arrived later, his new raincoat torn to shreds by the wind. And Harry found dozens of neighbors and friends there too. The house was packed!

The Maxson house was solid and well built. It seemed much safer than the smaller homes around it. It stood two stories tall, with four brick fireplaces anchoring it to the ground. "It was as if huge nails had been driven through the house from top to bottom," said Harry. "Before the storm was over we had about a hundred people in our house."

With the swift onslaught of the storm, families

living close to the beach had little time to evacuate. They had to make life-and-death decisions quickly. Even houses that seemed safe one minute were suddenly inundated by the terrific force of the water and swept away. Other houses shattered when floating timber and debris rammed into their walls, tearing them from their foundations.

Throughout the evening, Harry's mother moved from room to room, trying to reassure and comfort everyone. But she was worried about her next-door neighbors, who were expecting a new baby. She didn't think they were safe and asked Harry to go next door and bring the couple over to their house.

When Harry arrived, he found that his neighbor had just given birth to a baby boy. There was no way a new mom could wade through the fast-moving flood, made even more dangerous by fence posts, tree limbs, boards, and beams.

Harry had to come up with a solution—and fast.

"I returned home to get a ladder that some of the

men and myself used as a stretcher for the mother. The water at that time was about a waist high in her cottage, and the wind was getting terrific. It was with the greatest of difficulty that we moved her into our house and a comparatively safe bed."

While Harry rescued his neighbor, his dad was engaged in a desperate struggle to save the house from the pressure of the rising water. "Father anticipated what would happen to the house if the water got above the second floor level. It would float off," said Harry.

Soon, Harry, his dad, and some of their neighbors began to cut holes in the floor of each room. "We had no tools in the house, so we used pocket knives and butcher knives," Harry explained. "Each family was huddled together in corners under tables, so if the house went down they could all hang together."

Just as in Katherine Vedder's house, the main entrance posed a problem. Harry's house had double stained-glass-window front doors. To keep them from blowing in, Harry's father held one side closed, and a neighbor held the other shut. The men also took a table leaf from the dining room table and braced it under the front door handle to give added support to the door.

Each time a gust of wind struck, the house rattled something fierce. Flying timbers rammed into it like cannonballs. The houses and cottages around them were being ripped from their foundations. Telephone poles and trees toppled like toothpicks, tossed into the salty water surging through the city.

At about one in the morning, Harry's father sent him to the kitchen to open a window a few inches and listen for anyone calling out for help. Harry asked others to leave the kitchen so he could listen better.

He knelt by the window. "I heard what I didn't want to hear, a woman yelling, 'For God sake come and save us, our home is falling to pieces.' I shut the window as quickly as I could and tried to forget that woman's voice . . . it made me shake all over."

Harry didn't *want* to go out in the storm, but he couldn't ignore those cries for help. He asked several of the men to help him. Only one, a young newly married truck driver named Bill, was brave enough to go with the teen. Harry told his father they were leaving but didn't dare say anything to worry his mom.

Harry and Bill set out. They found a downed telephone pole floating along, and held on to it as they fought the rushing water. As they came closer to the house, they spotted the woman who had shouted for help perched precariously on the rooftop. She called out, telling them there were thirteen babies and children and about two dozen adults trapped in the attic.

Each gust of wind tore off part of the house, which had landed on railroad tracks. The house was crumbling fast. Time was running out.

Drawing nearer, Harry yelled to the people inside and asked each man to carry out a child. At first, there was silence. People were too scared to move.

Then one man emerged. He was African American, rescuing a white baby. One brave man was showing the way. Harry said, "I thanked him loud enough for all to hear and here they came—all the men with a baby each and some of their wives."

The bedraggled party set out, single file, each one grabbing on to the person in front. When Harry arrived with the first group, he found his mother in the kitchen making hot coffee and baking biscuits. He didn't record what she said, but she must have been relieved and proud of her brave son.

Then Harry went back for the next group. Everyone made it to the Maxsons' home alive.

Railroad tracks and railway cars in the aftermath of the Galveston hurricane.

WHAT CATEGORY STORM WAS THE GALVESTON HURRICANE?

In the United States, we use a scale called the **Saffir-Simpson Hurricane Wind Scale** to categorize hurricanes. The scale, developed in the 1970s, ranks storms from 1 to 5, based on a hurricane's maximum sustained, or constant, winds. The higher the category, the greater the hurricane's wind force and the potential danger the storm may cause.

A Category 5 storm has sustained winds greater than 156 mph. Winds in Category 4 are 130 up to 156 mph. Category 3 hurricanes range from 111 to 129 mph. Winds in Category 2 storms fall between 96 and 110 mph. And winds in Category 1 storms range from 74 to 95 mph.

Although the scale was not in use in 1900, based

on records and Isaac Cline's reports, experts believe Galveston was a Category 4 storm. Visit NOAA to read more about hurricane categories: https://www.nhc .noaa.gov/aboutsshws.php.

CHAPTER 7
Voices from the Storm

Annie: Just did get away!

Twenty-two-year-old Annie Smizer McCullough was a newlywed, proud of her house; her husband, Ed; and her garden. Early on Saturday, neighbors had gone to the beach to watch the big waves.

Annie and Ed lived on K Avenue and Eighth Street, not far and "near level with the beach," Annie recalled years later. Ed's cousin, Henry, a young teen, was staying with them. Annie was so worried about her roses, she asked Henry to dig them all up and stick them in a tub so they wouldn't get washed away.

But when Ed came back from an errand on Saturday, the family had more to worry about than rosebushes. As the weather worsened, they realized their house was far from safe. They decided to first head for the local African American school, East District School, on Tenth and Broadway. It wasn't far. So while Ed and Henry took the mule and the cart to pick up Annie's mother and other Smizer family members, Annie decided she'd just walk on over.

"When I got to corner of 9th and Broadway . . . the wind was so strong, and those waves comin', so I stopped. I didn't try to cross. Somebody picked me up, carried me across the street," said Annie.

But East District was just a frame building. When a neighbor came by with a big wagon used for delivering pianos, he announced he was heading for Rosenberg School, over on Tenth and I, which was larger and made of bricks. Annie and her family crowded on along with other friends. At times the water was so deep, the wagon was floating. The mules had to swim. Adults held on to children tightly.

"When we [hit] Rosenberg School, water hadn't come on there, but the *wind*! Ooh," exclaimed Annie more than sixty years later, recounting the tale to her

Many families sought refuge in public schools during the hurricane. The all-Black East District School was destroyed in the storm. Annie and Ed McCullough barely escaped being killed when part of the Rosenberg School, pictured here, collapsed.

great-niece Izola Collins. "Those men that was in the school, all they could do was stand up against those doors, try to hold them closed, keep them from blowin' open. . . . Upstairs, people was hollerin' and cryin', hunting their folk, couldn't find them. Oh, it was an awful thing! You want me to tell you. But no tongue can tell it!"

And then Ed urged Annie to move from one long hall to another. Suddenly, lightning struck the building's chimney. Bricks crashed down into the hall—instantly killing more than a dozen people. It was right in the hall, in the exact spot where Ed and Annie had been.

Annie never forgot it. "Just did get away!"

Milton: The House Fell on Us

On Saturday afternoon, about four o'clock, a young man named Milton Elford escaped from his house, with his parents and young nephew, Dwight. They made their way to a solid home in the neighborhood with a brick foundation. It was on higher ground and they hoped it would be safe.

As the storm roared, Milton's family clung to one another, along with fifteen or sixteen other people. Everyone clustered in one room.

"About 5 [o'clock] it grew worse and began to break up the fence, and the wreckage of other houses was coming against it," Milton wrote his brothers later. "We had it arranged that if the house showed signs of breaking up I would take the lead, and pa would come next, with Dwight and ma next."

Milton went on, "All at once the house went from its foundation and the water came in waist-deep, and we all made a break for the door, but could not get it open. We then smashed out the window and I led the way."

Too late. Milton said, "I had got only part way out when the house fell on us."

Everything happened fast. "I was hit on the head with something and it knocked me out and into the water head

Fifty-one people are reported to have died in this structure. Buildings that collapsed on people seeking shelter caused many deaths, including the members of Milton Elford's family.

first," Milton said. "I do not know how long I was down, as I must have been stunned. I came up and got hold of some wreckage on the other side of the house."

Milton was alone. He couldn't see anyone else. Not his parents or nephew. No one. "We must have all gone down the same time." Only he had come up. Milton could only guess the others had been thrown down under a wall or floor and pinned there. "It was just a wonder I did not get killed."

Milton had no choice: He had to keep going. He pushed his way out of the window, hoping his family would be right behind. Half swimming, half walking, he fought to get free of debris. He tried to keep from getting struck and dragged under again. At last he was out of the house. Partly running, partly swimming, Milton somehow made his way from one pile of debris to another.

"The street was full of tops and sides of houses, and the air was full of flying boards." Milton worried about getting trapped or hit or buried.

After about five blocks, Milton noticed the water beginning to go down. By now, it was about three in the morning.

It was too dark to see. Shivering and heartsick, Milton could only wait for dawn.

Arnold: Clinging to a Tree

Arnold R. Wolfram worked at a fruit and produce store in Galveston. Late Saturday afternoon, he headed home to his wife and children, about twenty blocks away. As he struggled to avoid flying glass and debris, Arnold came up with a brilliant idea. He'd just bought a new pair of shoes. Stepping into a doorway, he took them out of the package and tied them around his head for protection.

"At the corner I suddenly stopped in horror. A little Western Union messenger boy, a lad of about ten years, had fallen from his wheel [bicycle] into the street and was being swept by the water towards the sewer drain.

"Even as I started toward him, he was just going

into the whirlpool marking the spot of the drain. I caught him just in time, and dragged him up on the sidewalk."

Arnold recognized the boy as the son of neighbors. "I shouted to him above the roar of the wind and rain that I would take him home." Arnold's voice was lost in the gale, but he motioned for the young messenger to put his shoes around his head too.

"We were now forcing our way in the very face of the storm, which had become a raging tempest. It was almost impossible to shout above the din, and I realized then that we were facing death," said Arnold.

"The wind and rain were wreaking havoc everywhere, poles and wires were snapping, making passage down the street doubly dangerous; windows were crashing in; flimsy structures and parts of roofs were swirling swiftly down the river which had, just a few hours before, been a beautiful esplanaded street; and the water was rising higher every minute."

The next street had become a raging river. Arnold

Arnold Wolfram and his young neighbor clung to a tree to escape being swept away in a scene much like this one of raging floods during Hurricane Carol in Connecticut in August of 1954.

and the boy managed to swim across. On the other side, they spotted a man clinging to a fence, weak and exhausted. Before they could reach him, the man lost his grip and was swept away.

They kept on. The water now reached the boy's

armpits. As they waded across another street, the current surged. "We were both suddenly swept from our feet and rushed pell-mell into a tree. I struggled up to the surface all the while holding frantically to the tree," said Arnold.

Arnold looked around and was relieved to see the boy clinging on too. The two climbed higher up into the branches, shivering and holding on to the trunk for dear life. "The air was full of flying wood and slate and glass and the water was hurling everything imaginable at our perch," Arnold said. "During this time, we sat in our tree and prayed that we might be spared."

The moon peeked out behind the clouds. In its pale light, Arnold watched a terrifying scene unfold. A man and woman drifted toward them, clinging to the roof of a house. That makeshift raft crashed right into the tree. The man floated away on one part. The woman screamed and held out her hand. Arnold leaned out to grab her, but she was swept away.

"Our own situation was becoming more desperate," he said. Debris kept slamming against the tree, which wasn't very big. Arnold worried it would be torn up by the roots and they would be thrown into the deluge. They were exhausted and cold, and getting weaker by the minute. He wasn't sure how long they could hang on.

And then Arnold saw a way out. Some debris floated toward them and became lodged between the tree and the porch of the nearest house. Arnold's neighbors lived there. Arnold figured that if they moved fast, he and the boy could climb onto the debris and get to safety.

They made it! The neighbors welcomed the survivors with warm, dry clothes and hot food. It was now about midnight. The young messenger dropped off to sleep, but Arnold couldn't rest. He wanted the water to go down; he wanted to look for his wife and children.

He wanted this terrible night to be over.

Louise: "Wait!"

Seven-year-old Louise Bristol lived with her mom and siblings on Avenue C. This was a part of town closer to the bay and the Texas mainland, and farther from the Gulf beach. Louise was the baby of the family. Her sister, Lois, was eight years older and her brothers, John and William, were in their early twenties.

Louise's mom was a widow who struggled to make ends meet. She'd taken out a mortgage to enlarge the house so she could rent out rooms to boarders. Her home was her only way to support her family.

Even though they were farther from the Gulf shore, the floods still reached their neighborhood. At first, Louise was excited. "I remember seeing the water come down the street and being so delighted that we didn't have far to go to the beach. It was right there at the front door and then it began to get bigger and wider and was coming into the garden that my mother had."

Then, as Louise saw the garden disappear underwater,

she began to understand the danger. And by the time one of her older brothers reached home, the water was up to his chest.

Like Harry Maxson's father, Louise's mother was worried her house might crumble from the pressure of the flood. Louise said, "She got an axe and chopped holes into every floor of every room downstairs in the hallway and the kitchen and the dining room. So the water would come up into the house and hold the house on the ground."

The family gathered upstairs, bringing what they could from the kitchen cabinets. The house began to shake. At one point, Louise's sister screamed and pointed at a corner of the wall. It had separated from the ceiling and was moving up and down with each gust of wind.

Louise's mother didn't seem surprised. "She realized that the house was going to pieces around us," said Louise. "She knew that the back end had already gone off, because we heard the crash."

Now it was only a matter of time. They could see a lamp on in the house across the street, which was sturdier than theirs. Louise's mother had an idea. She took sheets off the bed and got ready to tie her children together. Her idea was that Louise's two brothers, who were strong swimmers, could pull the rest of the family across to the other house on a floating mattress.

Louise's fifteen-year-old sister urged her mom to hold off. "My mother would say, 'Let's go now.' My sister would say, 'Wait,'" said Louise.

"If we hadn't waited I'm sure we never would have made it across."

WHAT'S IN A NAME?

You might have noticed that, unlike Hurricane Katrina, Harvey, or Maria, the Galveston hurricane doesn't have a name.

That's because hurricanes weren't given names until 1953, when female names were used; starting in 1979, male and female names were used for Atlantic storms. NOAA's National Hurricane Center doesn't control the naming but follows a procedure established by the World Meteorological Organization, an agency of the United Nations.

The lists of names are recycled every six years, unless a name is retired and not used again. A name is retired if the storm is especially costly or deadly. To date, the most retired names happened in 2005. In addition to Katrina, that year saw Dennis, Rita, Stan, and Wilma. Each year's list contains twenty-one names. If there are more storms than that in any given year, names are taken from the Greek alphabet.

To see a list of hurricane names, visit the National Hurricane Center: https://www.nhc.noaa.gov/aboutnames.shtml.

Is your name on the list?

CHAPTER 8

The Cline Brothers: Drifting Out to Sea

By Saturday evening, more than fifty people had gathered in an upstairs room in Isaac Cline's house. At seven thirty, Isaac and Joseph had witnessed a sudden surge of four feet. The force of the water wreaked havoc on the houses near them, turning walls and roofs and furniture into battering rams against the Cline home.

Even a lighthouse on a rock couldn't hold out against the terrific beating. Joseph Cline tried to prepare the others for what he feared was about to happen.

"I urged them, if possible, to get on top of the drift and float upon it when the dangerous moment came," said Joseph. "As the peril became greater, so did the crowd's excitement. Most of them began to sing; some of them were weeping even wailing; while, again, others knelt in panic-stricken prayer."

And then it did happen.

Around eight thirty, the house began to topple over into the water. Joseph sprang into action. "I seized the hand of each of my brother's two children, turned my back toward the window, and, lunging from my heels, smashed through the glass and the wooden storm shutters, still gripping the hands of the two youngsters," he said.

Joseph had one goal in mind: to land on a wall resting on top of the water and not be crushed beneath the house as it fell. "The momentum hurled us all through the window as the building, with seeming deliberation, settled far over. It rocked a bit and then rose fairly level on the surface of the flood."

The plan worked. Joseph held on to Allie May, who was twelve, and Rosemary, eleven. "It was raining in torrents, and through winds of terrific force came flying pieces of timber. The clouds had broken in spots, and the dim light of the moon made it possible for us to see for a short distance over the mass of drift about us," said Joseph.

Joseph called out; no one answered. Then, just as the house began to break up completely, Joseph spotted Isaac and his youngest girl, six-year-old Esther, clinging to a drift a hundred feet away.

Isaac had been pushed under the water. As he groped for the surface, he'd brushed against Esther. He kept hold of her and managed to get to the surface and stay afloat by clinging to some debris. Cora Cline and her unborn child were lost, along with most everyone else who had been with them inside the house.

Now the survivors had to stay alive. It wouldn't be easy.

Throughout that long night, Isaac and Joseph, along with Isaac's three young daughters, struggled to keep afloat, clinging to one piece of wreckage after another. They would settle on some boards or planks that seemed safe. But before long, each makeshift raft would start to sink under their weight.

Some houses, like Isaac Cline's, capsized and disintegrated. This house on Avenue N was toppled on its side from the force of the water.

"We remained close together, climbing and crawling from one piece of wreckage to another," recalled Joseph.

In this way they floated, shivering and terrified. Minutes, then hours, went by. At one point, they were swept into the Gulf of Mexico into complete darkness. Would they drift so far out to sea they would be beyond reach? Would their raft hold together?

They were in luck. The wind shifted, blowing them back to Galveston Island. The brothers sat upright, trying to shelter the girls on their laps and protect them from flying timbers and drifting debris.

Once, incredibly, the family's dog appeared. The retriever sniffed each person in turn. Then, despite Joseph's best efforts to hold him, he jumped off the float again. Joseph realized the loyal dog was looking for his mistress, Cora, the only family member missing.

"I made a lunge for him, but he dodged, outran me, and plunged over the side of our drift. We never saw him any more," said Joseph.

The bulky wreckage was keeping the Cline family safe. At the same time, it made their unlikely lifeboat extremely dangerous to others. And soon they found themselves coming closer and closer to one house. Joseph heard people calling for help from inside.

He knew they were not bringing help, but destruction. In the next moment, their debris float struck the house with a crashing blow. The house began breaking apart.

"My brother was struck and knocked down by

one of the hurtling timbers," Joseph said later. After making sure Isaac was all right, Joseph noticed a little girl struggling in the water and plucked her out of the flood. In the darkness, he thought it was one of his nieces. But no, it was a survivor from the house. They later learned her name was Cora too. Now they were six drifting in the night.

Finally, about an hour before midnight, they floated near a house still standing on solid ground. This time, their raft lodged without damaging the structure.

"Tired and unspeakably battered, we climbed through an upstairs window into a room from which the roof and ceiling had been blown away," said Joseph. "Just under the floor of the room, the black waters of the Gulf were lapping. After having fought a frantic battle of body and mind for three hours, we dragged ourselves wearily inside."

Grateful to be alive, they joined other survivors in the house. They huddled together, hoping for this longest night to end.

Galveston survivors woke up to devastation after the storm.

Part Three
AFTER

Sunday Dawn & On

CHAPTER 9
Voices of Survivors

Katherine

Dawn. The wind had calmed. The waters were receding. But daylight brought unimaginable scenes of horror.

Everywhere they turned, Katherine Vedder and her family found chaos, death, and destruction. Nearly 3,000 homes had been completely swept out of existence; many more were damaged. And while the actual number of deaths can never be known, most historians estimate that at least 8,000 people were killed.

When Katherine's mother looked out the window on Sunday morning, the first thing she saw was the body of an African American child, tangled in the debris in their yard. Katherine and her mom would never forget that heartbreaking sight.

Only three houses still stood in Katherine's entire neighborhood. Katherine's brother called out, "'Papa, where are the Peeks?'"

They looked over to the spot where their neighbors' house had been—the house Katherine's father had thought was sturdier than their own, the house he had planned to go to for refuge if theirs didn't survive.

"Not a plank nor brick remained," said Katherine. "Not even a trace of the foundation. Richard Peek, his wife, eight children, and two servants were gone." Their bodies were never found.

The Vedder home was too damaged to live in, so the family set out on the grim walk to Katherine's grandparents, hoping they had survived. It took five hours to get through what had once been a thriving city. Katherine's father carried her much of the way. Debris blocked their passage almost everywhere.

"No streets or roads were visible. The wreckage piled high obscured every familiar landmark," recalled Katherine. "We picked our way where we could, sometimes in ankle-deep water and mud, sometimes in water waist deep where great holes had been created by the current."

They came across many bodies: a small white child wrapped in a quilt, a nun who had tied several children to her body, a Black man caught in the mud with his bicycle. People who had tried to run, to get to higher ground, to swim, or even to ride a bicycle to safety. All lost. At one point, Katherine's mother broke down and wept.

Katherine's grandparents lived in the center of town, farther from the beach. Fortunately, they'd come through fine, and their house had weathered the storm. It was eleven days before Katherine's parents returned home to see what could be salvaged. Her mother found three dozen pieces of her wedding china, buried in the soft mud and without a chip on them.

Afterward, Katherine and her siblings were sent to New York to live with her other grandparents while the family home was being repaired. She later returned to live in Galveston. Katherine grew up to study music in college. She married, and became active in the Galveston Historical Society.

Katherine never forgot that night and the rescue of her kitten and the baby. Years later, traveling on a bus, she found herself sitting next to a young woman. When the woman learned Katherine was from Galveston, she mentioned that her grandmother had also lived through the storm.

The young woman said, "'You know, my grandmother told me the most fantastic story. She told me about a home down the island where a lot of people spent the night of the storm and there was a little baby that was brought in just about dead and the lady who lived in the home saved the little baby. . . . Isn't that the most remarkable thing?'"

Katherine replied, "'Well, you don't know how remarkable it is, because it was in my home that the baby was saved and it was my mother who saved him.'"

And, of course, the kitten helped too.

Arnold

At midnight on Saturday, Arnold Wolfram had managed to save himself and a boy from his neighborhood by clambering over floating debris to reach the porch of a house. After eating and getting a change of clothes, the boy dropped off to sleep.

Not Arnold. All he could think of was his wife and four children at home. Had they survived?

At first light on Sunday morning, he set out to find them. His first inkling of the extent of the desolation came almost instantly. Stepping into the water that still covered the street, his foot hit something soft. Reaching under the water, Arnold realized he had stepped on a dead body. "I turned away sick and horrified, but as I walked on, again and again, I saw bodies of men, women and children, everywhere."

Arnold quickened his pace, trying to make his way through the wreckage, his fears rising. Finally, he reached his own block. "I dreaded to look but finally did—Oh my God, where would I find my loved ones—for I saw that my home was tilted crazily, the roof crushed in.

"I stood stunned, sickened to the very core of my being. Finally I started forward for I knew that no matter what I might find on reaching the house, I had to search those ruins for all I had held dear."

Then Arnold heard someone call his name. A friend had come to look for him and reported that Arnold's wife and children were safe. They'd escaped from the house when it started to sway and shake and managed to survive inside a grocery store on the next corner.

Arnold and his family lost much of what they owned but eventually were able to rebuild their house. Nearly forty years later, when he was almost eighty-one, Arnold reflected, "The little lad whom I saved is now grown and married and has a very good business in another state but we still correspond. . . . All my children have grown up, married, and have children of their own. And I even have some few great-grandchildren.

"But with all the changes of the years, that one night has always remained most vivid in my mind."

Annie

Annie Smizer McCullough and her husband, Ed, had barely escaped with their lives when part of the Rosenberg School collapsed. When the moon came out and the water began to run off, they headed for the courthouse, which became a makeshift shelter for many.

Izola Collins's maternal grandfather, Ralph "Papa" Scull, brought his family to the courthouse too. Izola's mother, Viola, was twelve. She had one especially vivid memory of the storm. Viola recalled leaving home to go to the courthouse on Saturday as the storm worsened. "She told me emphatically, that as Papa called to her to go, she looked up and saw a huge wave, bigger than she had ever seen, rolling toward them."

Many in Galveston flocked to public buildings

A survivor amid the wreckage. Entire blocks on the Gulf side of Galveston were destroyed. Most buildings were damaged, leaving thousands homeless.

during the hurricane. A Black laborer named Henry Johnson had moved to Galveston just before the storm and lived in a boardinghouse. When it struck, he escaped to the Union Passenger Depot, a sturdier brick building. The boardinghouse was totally destroyed. Like thousands of others, Henry was left homeless.

Annie and Ed McCullough stayed at the courthouse for a week after the storm. There they met a white man who offered the young couple a place to stay. Along with Ed's mother and two brothers, Annie and Ed moved into the house's servants' quarters until they could go to relatives in Hallettsville, Texas. Before then, however, "These white people just turned their place over to us," remembered Annie.

Not everyone was kind, though. And racism had not gone away. Izola Collins interviewed her neighbor, Joseph "Joe" Arnold Banks, whose grandfather had lived through the hurricane. Joe's grandfather said that as he and others were fleeing the rising waters in a wagon, they tried to rescue a white woman in the

A young survivor happy to be alive.

water. But because the people in the wagon were Black, the woman pulled back and refused.

The courthouse sheltered all who came. Joe Banks's grandfather remembered that at least for a short time, people there faced the hurricane together.

Milton

Milton and his parents and young nephew had been caught together in a house that collapsed. Milton was the only one who made it out. Sunday dawn found him bruised, shocked, and sore. "As soon as it was light enough I went back to the location of the house, and not a sign of it could be found, and not a sign of any house within two blocks, where before there was scarcely a vacant lot."

He had five dollars in his pocket and the clothes he was wearing. "It seems that I have been dazed," Milton Elford wrote to his brothers on Thursday, five days later. "I have not been able to collect my thoughts until today. I have not found any of the remains yet."

Milton wasn't the only traumatized survivor wandering helplessly in the midst of the rubble of what had been prosperous Galveston. Where houses had stood, full of laughter and family life, there was only destruction. Nothing looked the same. The city—or what had been the city—was nearly gone.

"There are hundreds of houses in one heap, and you can scarcely recognize a single piece," Milton wrote. "For three to five blocks wide and for about four miles, solid blocks of dwellings and hotels and the residence part of the city, there is not a vestige—not a board. It is all swept clean and banked up in a pile reaching all around from bay to beach."

There was little time to grieve. Milton was soon put to work uncovering the remains of the storm's thousands of victims and burying them. He still hoped to find his family and give them a proper burial.

"I have been helping clear away the debris . . . where we are most likely to find them," Milton told his brothers. "There are hundreds of men working there but the work moves on slowly . . . It is an awful sight. Every few minutes, somewhere within a block of us they find dead bodies, and often where there is one there are more. Yesterday we took out twelve from one spot. It was a large house, and they had gathered there for safety, and all died together, wedged in between ceiling and floor."

Galveston was under martial law, with white soldiers patrolling to prevent looting and stealing. African American men in particular were pressed into service to handle the grisly task of removing the bodies of victims. They weren't allowed to refuse. "The law would come to your house," remembered Annie Smizer McCullough.

It was gruesome work. Yet the heat, odor, and fear of disease made it imperative to act as soon as possible. With such overwhelming numbers of victims, some bodies had to be burned. Other corpses were hauled out to sea. There was no chance to mourn or to have proper funerals. No chance for the survivors to say goodbye. The chaos made it more difficult to track friends or family, or compile a complete list of the dead.

"It is the most awful thing of the kind that has ever happened in history," said Milton. "Hundreds of families have gone down, and not a sign of anything left of them."

With all the destruction around him, Milton couldn't stop thinking of what he might have done differently, how he might have saved his family. He replayed the final terrible moments as the house collapsed and the water rushed in; he thought of the people wild with fright, the water rising higher and higher as they fought to get out.

But the end was the same. Milton's parents and nephew were gone. At least, Milton told his brothers, "It was all over in a second. I am satisfied they did not fear death in the least, and I do not believe they suffered." That was his only consolation.

Louise

Since Louise Bristol was only seven, her mother tried to protect her from the horrible sights and smells in the aftermath of the storm. Louise wasn't allowed to leave the house. She knew things were bad, though.

Her two older brothers were pressed into service to remove the dead. "They were told they must help and then they were told they had to dig," Louise recalled. "There was no identification and no prayers said or anything else, the bodies were just put in the ground. There were so many of them that they couldn't find any more ground to bury them. They took them out to sea and then they washed back in again, so they had to be burned."

Louise was also old enough to understand that the hurricane had made life much harder for her mom, who'd lost so much. Their house was almost completely destroyed.

"We went out to the porch to look at our house,

because the back end of it had completely collapsed and it was in the yard next door. Everything, cook stove, the two bedrooms with all the furniture and all the dining room furniture and everything was in the yard next door.

"I can remember crying the next day. We had plenty to eat, because she'd [my mother had] gotten all the food upstairs. But I was crying because it was raining in my beans and I couldn't stop it from raining. I remember a silly little thing like that."

Louise later worked for the railroad and married, becoming a mother, grandmother, and great-grandmother. She often visited public schools to talk about history and the Galveston hurricane. She died in Houston in 1987 at the age of ninety-four.

Harry

"What a wreck it left," said fourteen-year-old Harry Maxson. "Houses split half in two, others gone entirely and cisterns everywhere with all kinds of furniture, bales of cotton and most everything floating all around."

He never got the names of everyone saved in his parents' home that night. But Harry guessed that, all told, they'd sheltered about 150 people, along with several dogs, cats, and even pet birds.

In the aftermath, Harry's mother was trying to feed these homeless survivors. The chief of police arranged for Harry to pick up some extra food supplies—canned salmon, potatoes, flour, and lard.

They ate canned salmon for ten days. After that, Harry said, he never wanted to eat it again.

On Sunday afternoon, Harry walked around town looking for his friends from school. Some had made it. Others were missing or had died. "About 35th and Avenue P or Q, I saw a lot of men starting small fires and before I knew what had happened I had been conscripted to help bury or burn the dead," he said.

"It was too gruesome to describe the condition some of these bodies were in. In less than an hour I looked up

Horse-drawn carts for food delivery are protected by armed guards in the aftermath of the disaster.

and saw Col. McCaleb, an officer of the Local Militia. He said, 'Harry, you're big enough, but too young to be doing this kind of job.' He wrote me out a pass and told me to go home which I was awfully glad to do."

But before he got home, Harry came across the bodies of twin boys, about five years old, still clinging to each other. He fetched a shovel and buried them. Not far away, he saw the corpse of a woman, with a man sitting next to her. The man had been looking for his wife all day.

Harry said, "I tried to get him to go on, but he wanted to stay and help me lay her away . . . he just kept mumbling her name. After getting the grave dug large enough, I found a corrugated washing board and he helped me lay her in her grave so tenderly. It was pitiful! I put the washboard on her face and refilled the grave. Then he thanked me and walked south toward the gulf. I never saw him again."

Brave Harry Maxson lived until he was eighty-one.

When he died in April of 1967, his written account of the storm was discovered among his personal papers.

He closed his recollections this way: "Many of my friends on hearing I passed through the Big 1900 Galveston Storm wanted to hear all about the details— and it was such a long sad story, I made the habit of telling it only once a year and that, of course, would be on Thanksgiving Day."

BE PREPARED!

While people in Galveston had no warning, experts today recommend that families have a preparation kit for emergencies, whether it's a hurricane, wildfire, flood, blizzard, or public health crisis. It's always good to be prepared.

There are different kinds of emergencies. Sometimes, families must leave home immediately to escape danger. Other times, it might be possible to bring a few belongings with you. While our possessions mean a lot, the most important thing is safety. It's critical to follow the guidance of local police, firefighters, or other officials whose job is to keep citizens safe.

And even if the adults in your home are the ones who assemble a preparation kit, everyone has a role to play. You should listen carefully to directions, and if the emergency means your family should stay home, you should know where supplies are and follow directions about using them.

FEMA, the Federal Emergency Management Agency, a part of the United States government, has an Emergency Supplies Checklist for Kids online with ideas for a scavenger hunt to help your family build a kit.

Most experts advise including flashlights, batteries, candles and matches (only for adults to use), a first aid kit, toothbrushes and toothpaste, pet food, water, a pair of shoes, and clothes for three days, among other supplies.

Check it out at: https://www.fema.gov/media-library-data/35f3ff58f7cc6a2047fdb1e8bae8466b/FEMA_checklist_child_508_071513.pdf.

CHAPTER 10
Too Many Bodies

After Isaac Cline's house fell over into the surging seas, the Cline brothers had been swept into the Gulf of Mexico, balanced precariously on debris. It was all they could do to keep Isaac's three daughters from falling into the water. Luckily, when the wind blew them back to town, they were able to clamber into a house to wait out the rest of the storm.

The girls had survived, but their mother had died. The body of Cora Cline wasn't found for days, and could be identified only by her diamond engagement ring.

On Sunday morning, the Clines ventured out. Like everyone else, they were shocked by the number of victims. Piles of debris ten feet deep stretched on and on for blocks. Sand covered what had once been streets.

Joseph stood on top of a pile of wreckage and surveyed the wasteland around him. "Not a house was left standing in the area ravaged by the flood, nor could a single street be outlined by the eye. The exact number of the dead was never known, because so many of the bodies were washed away."

There was one bright spot for Joseph. In the middle of the night, he'd plucked from the flood a seven-year-old also named Cora. The little girl told Joseph she lived in San Antonio, Texas, and had been visiting Galveston with her mom and brother. Joseph left Cora in the care of the people in the house where the Clines had spent the last hours of the storm.

Several days later, Joseph happened to overhear a grief-stricken man searching for his lost family. He had come from San Antonio to try to find them.

"Acting upon a sudden impulse, I drew nearer

and asked him if he knew a little girl named Cora Goldbeck," Joseph said. "I shall never forget his face, lined with dread and horror, as he replied, 'She is my daughter.'

"'Then your daughter is safe,' I told him." Though Cora Goldbeck survived, her mother and brother were lost.

Joseph had a footnote to this story. "Many years later, a sequel to this episode brought great happiness to my wife and to me. Miss Cora Goldbeck, a young lady of nineteen, visited us in our home at Corpus Christi [Texas], where she had come in person to thank me for saving her life. The lovely little girl had become a beautiful young woman." Cora lived to be ninety-four years old.

Cora Goldbeck and her father were lucky to find each other. Locating relatives, victims, and survivors after the storm was difficult. So many people had died—sometimes entire families—that it wasn't possible to identify them.

Too Many Bodies

There were just too many.

Outsiders who came to Galveston after the hurricane were overwhelmed by the devastation. Thomas Monagan was one of the first people from off the island to arrive. He worked for an insurance company. He and some colleagues set out on Sunday from Dallas to assess the damages their company would need to cover.

Thomas and his group couldn't get the entire way by train because of damage to the tracks, so they found a sailboat to take them across the bay to Galveston Island. They spotted furniture, debris, and even dead bodies floating in the water. It was dark when they got close to the city, so they anchored offshore on Sunday night.

The very first man they met on Monday morning told them hundreds of bodies were already being burned. Thomas didn't believe it. Surely, the man must be exaggerating. "But we investigated and found it to be true. The authorities were piling up the bodies on the debris and setting fire to the whole mass."

The mortuaries had filled quickly, but there were still thousands of victims. "So they had brought in abandoned barges to the wharf and loaded on them hundreds of bodies as they were pulled from the wreckage of destroyed buildings," said Thomas. "Most of these were badly discolored and unrecognizable. They tied sash weights to their legs and threw them into the bay and came back for another load."

The horrors didn't end there. "We walked over the island, speechless at the sight of the prosperous city laid in waste."

In this desperate situation, where could people turn for help?

Today, after natural disasters, the federal government provides help through FEMA, the Federal Emergency Management Agency. Nonprofit organizations such as the American Red Cross also step in to help. And in 1900, the woman who founded the American Red Cross was still alive. Her name was Clara Barton.

Born in 1821, Clara was almost seventy-nine when the deadliest hurricane struck. Nearly forty years earlier, she had rushed to nurse soldiers on Civil War battlefields. And she established the American Red Cross in 1881. Disaster relief was what she knew best.

Despite her age and ill health, Clara came to Galveston's aid. She and six helpers arrived on September 15, about a week after the hurricane, when smoke from piles of burning rubble and bodies still enveloped the city. Clara stayed for two months, often directing operations from a couch in her hotel room when she didn't feel well.

Clara and her team set up a local chapter of the Red Cross and organized people into sections to help with temporary shelter, clothing, orphaned children, and a soup kitchen. Clara Barton's reputation also helped bring awareness to Galveston's plight.

Newspapers carried stories about the deadly hurricane and the devastated survivors. Ordinary people in America and in other countries too contributed money and goods. Donors in the state of New York contributed more than $90,000. Seven-year-old Louise Bristol remembered getting a new outfit in a box of clothes from the north.

African American organizations responded as well. H. C. Bell, of Denton, Texas, served as Grand Master of the Colored Odd Fellows, a civic group. He appealed for gifts to benefit all victims: "'To the Lodges and Members of the Grand United Order of Odd Fellows in Texas: Dear Brethren—The greatest calamity that has ever visited any city in America visited Galveston on the 8th . . . leaving in its wake thousands of dead and helpless people of our race, together with the white race.

"'It is our duty to help, as far as we are able, to relieve the suffering condition of the citizens of Galveston. It goes without saying that the white citizens of Texas have always contributed freely to ameliorate and alleviate suffering humanity; it is, therefore, our bounden duty, and, indeed, this is a most fitting opportunity for us, as members of the greatest negro organization in the world, to show to our white fellow-citizens of Texas the charitable spirit that has always characterized Odd Fellows.'"

Rebuilding the city of Galveston was a slow process. A Central Relief Committee set up a subcommittee to repair and construct new houses. Close to $300,000 was used for new housing, which in today's dollars is about ten million.

In May of 1902, the housing subcommittee reported that more than four hundred cottages had been completed at a cost of about $300 each: "'Contracts were made for building three-room cottages (as fast as men and materials were available) on lots belonging to families whose residences had been entirely destroyed. No distinction was made between the races.'" Cash contributions also helped about eleven hundred families repair or rebuild their houses.

Since preference was given to people who already owned their homes, poorer families and those who

After the storm, thousands were left homeless and forced into makeshift structures such as this.

rented Galveston's alley houses, many occupied by Black residents, were often left out. Some people simply decided to leave. Historians estimate about 2,000 people moved away from Galveston, while others constructed makeshift dwellings.

While Galveston worked to try to meet immediate needs, the hurricane prompted action for the future. This was the deadliest natural disaster in American history and it could not be allowed to happen again.

First, Galveston tried to protect houses by raising the land where most residents lived, by about eight feet above sea level. Then, to help protect the city from storm surges in future storms, Galveston built a thick concrete seawall seventeen feet high along the Gulf shore. The Galveston Seawall, completed in 1904 (and since extended from about three miles to ten miles), is listed on the National Register of Historic Places.

In 1915, another hurricane struck Galveston. Although there was some damage, the concrete barrier held back the storm surge.

In Cuba, it was now clear that Father Gangoite had been correct; the ban on Cuban weather cables was removed.

Joseph Cline married Ula Jackson in 1901, when he was thirty-one. He remained in the weather service in Dallas, Texas, but never forgot the Galveston storm and its "night of horror."

Isaac Cline tried to pick up the pieces of his life and make a future for himself and his three daughters. In 1901, Willis Moore, still in charge of the Weather Bureau, transferred Isaac to New Orleans. There, Isaac devoted himself to trying to understand hurricanes and became a national expert on these deadly storms. He did not remarry.

As for the city of Galveston, it never reclaimed its former glory. And the survivors of the deadliest hurricane in America would never be the same.

EPILOGUE

Hurricanes: Yesterday, Today, and Tomorrow

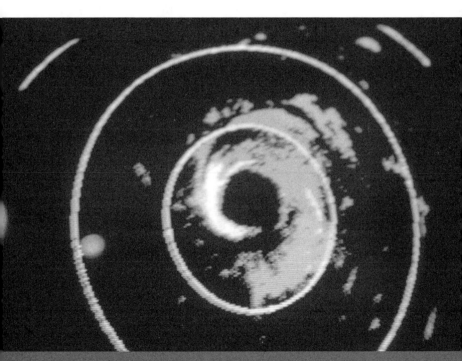

Aircraft radar display of the center of Hurricane Frederic in 1979, which caused an estimated 1.7 billion dollars in damage.

Other Deadly Hurricanes of the Past

Hurricanes are the most expensive, frequent, and deadly natural disasters in the world. These giant whirlwinds have terrified human beings for as long as we have existed—and now, in the twenty-first century, with warming ocean temperatures, hurricanes have the potential to become even more dangerous.

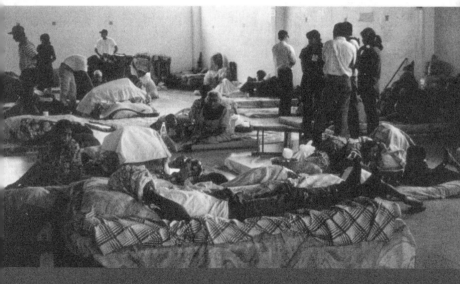

Shelter for the homeless in the wake of Hurricane Mitch, a Category 5 storm that struck Honduras in October of 1998, causing more than 7,000 deaths and more than five billion dollars in damage.

The Galveston hurricane, in which more than 8,000 people lost their lives, remains the worst natural disaster causing loss of life in the United States. But world history is full of examples of horrific and deadly storms.

In 1737, a cyclone struck India, killing more than 300,000; in 1865, again in India, another cyclone killed 50–70,000 people. In 1897, more than 175,000 people died as a result of a cyclone in Bengal, which is now Bangladesh.

The aftereffects of storms often bring more deaths, when food supplies and water sources are disrupted. In 1876, a storm in Bengal killed 100,000 people, with the same number dying later from hunger and disease.

Atlantic hurricanes have also caused tremendous loss of life. Twenty-two thousand people died during a hurricane in the Caribbean in 1780. In 1928, the Okeechobee hurricane killed 1,500 people in the Caribbean before striking Florida, where 3,000 more people lost their lives.

Other hurricanes have caused massive amounts of damage even though their death tolls have not been as horrific. A chart in the back of this book lists the ten most damaging hurricanes in the United States to date.

Hurricane Katrina, 2005

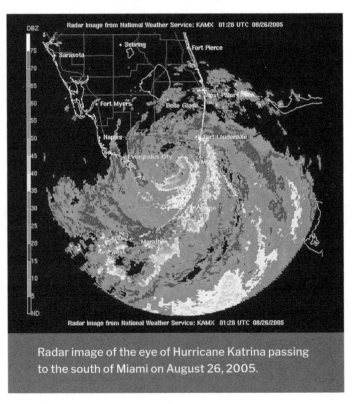

Radar image of the eye of Hurricane Katrina passing to the south of Miami on August 26, 2005.

Despite better hurricane tracking, we continue to experience deadly hurricanes in the United States and in the U.S. territory of Puerto Rico. On Monday, August 29, 2005, Hurricane Katrina slammed into New Orleans and the Gulf Coast. Like the Galveston hurricane in 1900, the storm's path took it across the Gulf of Mexico.

Two days before, at five o'clock on the morning of Saturday, August 27, the National Hurricane Center had released an advisory that the Category 3 Hurricane Katrina, which had already hit Florida as a Category 1 storm, was gaining strength.

As Katrina traveled across the warm waters of the Gulf, the storm intensified just as the Galveston hurricane had. At one point, wind gusts reached more than 170 miles per hour. Katrina made landfall again on Monday morning as a Category 3 storm, causing damage to beachfront areas in Mississippi and Alabama, as well as Louisiana, where it caused the most damage and loss of life.

The inside of a school cafeteria in Mississippi after Hurricane Katrina in 2005, with mud left on tables and stools after the water receded.

Katrina will always be remembered for its devastating impact on the vibrant, historic city of New Orleans and its residents, many of whom are people of color. Much of the city is below sea level. It was not the hurricane's winds, but rainfall and the hurricane's storm surge that resulted in disaster. Water overwhelmed the city's levee system—barriers designed to contain the waters of nearby Lake Pontchartrain and Lake Borgne.

On Monday afternoon, about 20 percent of the entire city was submerged; by the next day, about 80 percent was underwater.

While an evacuation order had been issued for New Orleans, many people accustomed to storms battering their city simply didn't realize the severity of the situation and didn't leave. Others had no means to evacuate. Hospitals and nursing homes struggled to respond.

As the waters rose and overwhelmed the levees, disaster unfolded. Some residents were stranded on

Barbershop in New Orleans damaged by Katrina.

rooftops, desperate for rescue by helicopter or boat. Local emergency services couldn't keep up.

With no place to shelter, about 9,000 people (and later as many as 15,000 to 20,000) converged on the Louisiana Superdome, a large domed stadium. Local officials were overwhelmed. Federal government relief efforts were inadequate and slow. Meanwhile, desperate families suffered in terrible conditions in the Superdome, without adequate water, food, medicine, or supplies.

The horror of Katrina and the suffering it caused for so many families became a symbol of the failure of government preparedness. Thousands of survivors were forced to relocate, moving to other cities to try to remake their lives.

Hurricane Katrina ranks alongside Hurricane Harvey in 2017 as the costliest hurricane in America; each caused a staggering $125 billion in damage. But the greatest tragedy of Katrina was the loss of life:

Only steps are left of this structure after Hurricane Katrina struck Mississippi.

More than 1,800 people died. Americans were angry and devastated and they raised important questions about why this tragedy happened. They also asked: More than one hundred years after Galveston, how can we better protect all people against deadly storms?

Hurricane Maria, 2017

Hurricane Katrina isn't the most recent deadly hurricane. On Wednesday, September 20, 2017, a Category 5 hurricane called Maria hit the U.S. territory of Puerto Rico, along with other islands, especially Dominica and St. Croix. Causing more than ninety billion dollars in damage to houses, roads, and utilities, Maria is the third-costliest hurricane in U.S. history—with high winds and floods devastating much of Puerto Rico—behind Hurricane Katrina in 2005 and Hurricane Harvey, which hit Texas, also in 2017, and caused widespread flooding and sixty-eight deaths.

However, unlike Galveston, where most deaths occurred during the storm, many of the deaths from Hurricane Maria occurred afterward, and weren't included in the original official death toll. There are several reasons for this.

Hurricane Maria knocked out the island's power system, which was not robust. NOAA estimated that 80 percent of Puerto Rico's utility poles and transmission lines were damaged. The system also took a very long time to repair.

By the end of January of 2018, several months after the storm, only 65 percent of Puerto Rico's 3.4 million residents had power. This meant that for months after the storm, most residents had no electricity, water, or phone service. These conditions caused severe problems, and also led to illness and death. People could not refrigerate medicine, contact relatives or emergency services, or get to the doctor.

As a result, Maria proved even more deadly than Hurricane Katrina. Reports of those who died because of the hurricane have varied, but most experts attribute more than 2,900 deaths to the disaster.

WANT TO BECOME A METEOROLOGIST OR CLIMATOLOGIST?

Meteorologists use math and science to help predict the weather. They work in many different kinds of organizations, from large agencies like NOAA to local television stations. You might see weather forecasters on the nightly news. Other scientists study storms or climate change. They do research, provide forecasts, and apply their skills to new satellite technologies and weather models. To learn more, visit: https://www.environmentalscience.org/career/meteorologist.

The Future: Hurricanes and Global Warming

Hurricanes have always been a part of Earth's climate system. However, scientists have determined that intense hurricane activity has increased in the North Atlantic over the last fifty years.

Why? The reason is human-caused **global warming**.

The global climate crisis has been caused by burning fossil fuels, like oil and coal, to run factories, cars, and airplanes. As they burn, these fuels emit carbon dioxide, which gets trapped in the Earth's atmosphere. This creates a **greenhouse effect**. It's called that because these gases trap the sun's radiation and make the Earth warmer, the same way a glass greenhouse creates warmth for plants.

Global warming is an example of a greenhouse effect. Because the atmosphere is warmer, glaciers and pack ice melt into the oceans, which also have higher temperatures. Sea levels rise, and coastal areas and cities are in more danger from storm surges and flooding.

Climatologists who study the effects of global

warming conclude that while there might not be more frequent hurricanes, these deadly storms will probably have stronger winds and bring more rain. For instance, in 2017, Hurricane Harvey dropped more than forty inches of rain in four days on Texas, causing widespread flooding and dozens of deaths in the Houston area.

NOAA predicts that worldwide, intense tropical cyclones in Categories 4 and 5 will increase throughout the twenty-first century.

Hurricanes are here to stay. But we can take action to lessen the threat to people, birds and animals, and entire cities. The challenge of creating a society based on renewable energy and creating a world not dependent on fossil fuels lies before us.

It is the greatest challenge of all.

THE GREAT GALVESTON HURRICANE FACTS & FIGURES

Date: Saturday, September 8, 1900

Place: Galveston, Texas

City population: 37,789

Estimated winds: 130–140 mph

Storm surge: 15 feet or higher

Estimated deaths: 8,000 or more (true number unknown)

Damage: $20 million (equivalent to about $700 million today)

Houses destroyed: 2,636

People left homeless: More than 4,000

Aftermath: Over the next ten years, the city built a ten-mile-long seawall, about seventeen feet high and sixteen feet at the base. About 500 city blocks were raised an average of eight feet.

In 1915, Galveston was hit by another hurricane. The seawall held and within the city only six people perished.

More for Young Weather Scientists

GLOSSARY

AIR PRESSURE

Also called atmospheric pressure, the pressure of the atmosphere exerted on the Earth.

BAROMETER

Instrument to measure barometric or air pressure.

EYE

Area in the center of a tropical cyclone with low air pressure and calm winds.

EYEWALL

A ring of spiraling clouds and winds whirling around the eye of a storm.

GLOBAL WARMING

A gradual increase in the atmosphere's temperature.

GOES

NOAA's Geostationary Operational Environmental Satellite.

GREENHOUSE EFFECT

The trapping of the sun's warmth in the lower atmosphere, caused by release of gases like carbon dioxide from burning fuels such as gas and coal.

HURRICANE

A tropical cyclone with winds over 74 mph in the North Atlantic, Northeast Pacific Ocean east of the International Date Line, or the South Pacific Ocean east of 160 degrees.

HURRICANE SEASON

Time of year, June 1 to November 30, when storms are most likely to form in the North Atlantic.

HURRICANE WARNING

An announcement that a hurricane is expected.

HURRICANE WATCH

An announcement that a hurricane may possibly be approaching.

METEOROLOGY

Science concerned with the atmosphere and forecasting weather.

NOAA

National Oceanic and Atmospheric Administration, part of the U.S. government.

RADAR

Radar stands for RAdio Detection And Ranging. In use since World War II, this technology helps weather science detect precipitation and forecast storms.

SAFFIR-SIMPSON HURRICANE WIND SCALE

A scale of 1 to 5 used to indicate a storm's intensity and the likelihood of storm damage.

From NOAA:

CATEGORY	WIND SPEED (MPH)	DAMAGE
1	74–95	Very dangerous winds will produce some damage
2	96–110	Extremely dangerous winds will cause extensive damage
3	111–129	Devastating damage will occur
4	130–156	Catastrophic damage will occur
5	>156	Catastrophic damage will occur

Glossary

SEAWALL

A wall or embankment used as a barrier to protect people and things on land from erosion or water coming from the sea.

STORM SURGE

An abnormal rise in sea level with water pushed onto land by the force of a severe storm.

SWELL

A series of waves generated by distant weather systems.

TROPICAL CYCLONE

General meteorological term used to describe storms that form in the tropics with winds that circulate around a center.

TROPICAL DEPRESSION

A tropical cyclone with a maximum sustained wind speed of 38 mph or less.

TROPICAL STORM

A tropical cyclone with wind speeds of 39–73 mph.

TROPICAL WAVE

An area of low pressure and storms moving east to west. May also be called easterly wave or African easterly wave.

TROPICS

Region of the globe surrounding the equator.

TYPHOON

A severe storm, with winds over 74 mph, that forms in the Northwest Pacific Ocean, west of the International Date Line.

WEATHER SATELLITE

An object that orbits above the Earth and monitors weather and climate, using sophisticated imaging equipment. Geostationary satellites appear to hover in place, as they move at the same speed and direction as the Earth's rotation.

TEST YOUR KNOWLEDGE

Fill in the Correct Words

_____: The center of a hurricane, with calm winds.

_____: A tropical cyclone with winds 74 mph or more in the North Atlantic, Northeast Pacific Ocean east of the International Date Line, or the South Pacific Ocean east of 160 degrees.

_____: A rise in sea level pushing water onshore in a severe storm.

_____: A severe storm, with winds over 74 mph, that forms in the Northwest Pacific Ocean, west of the International Date Line.

The Deadliest Hurricanes Then and Now

_____: Instrument to measure air pressure.

_____: A ring of spiraling clouds and winds whirling around the eye of a storm.

_____: Science concerned with the atmosphere and forecasting weather.

_____: Scale used to measure a hurricane's intensity.

ANSWERS:
EYE
HURRICANE
STORM SURGE
TYPHOON
BAROMETER
EYEWALL
METEOROLOGY
SAFFIR-SIMPSON HURRICANE WIND SCALE

HURRICANE WORD UNSCRAMBLE

LELSW

YCLENOC

LTICRPOA

YTAOGREC

The Deadliest Hurricanes Then and Now

ANSMTIU

PEAMSOETHR

PHONYTO

LSEITLAET

LEWYELA

ANSWERS: SWELL, CYCLONE, TROPICAL, CATEGORY, TSUNAMI, ATMOSPHERE, TYPHOON, SATELLITE, EYEWALL

MORE HURRICANE ACTIVITIES

Make a Barometer

Weather forecasters use barometers to measure air pressure. Visit Scholastic online to make your own.

» https://www.scholastic.com/teachers/articles /teaching-content/barometer

Track a Hurricane

Follow along with a NOAA lesson plan to track a hurricane.

» https://aambcelebrating200.blob.core.windows. net/celebrating200-prod/media/edufun/book /FollowthatHurricane.pdf

Get a Hurricane Tracking Chart

Download and print a hurricane tracking chart from the National Hurricane Center at NOAA.

» https://www.nhc.noaa.gov/AT_Track_chart.pdf

Perform a Hurricane Katrina Damage Assessment Activity

Using maps and aerial photography images online.

» https://oceanservice.noaa.gov/education/lessons /katrina.html

SAMPLE ORAL HISTORY QUESTIONS

Stories matter! Often, oral history interviews are conducted by recording the interview with audio or video. Afterward, someone writes up the interview; this is called a transcript. You can also make your own oral history question sheet and leave blanks to write the person's responses. Try to capture their words exactly. Here are some ideas for an oral history interview with a grandparent.

Please state your full name and date of birth.

Where were you born and what are the names of your parents and siblings?

The Deadliest Hurricanes Then and Now

What was your house like when you were a child and what did you like to do with your family?

What is your favorite memory from when you were young?

Where did you go to school and what did you dream of doing?

When did you get married and to whom?

Have you lived through a difficult time in your life or a big storm or hurricane?

How did you get through hard times? What gives you hope?

What advice do you have for young people today?

TIMETABLE OF
MAJOR U.S. HURRICANES

Throughout recorded history, hurricanes and cyclones have proven deadly in many parts of the world. Here are a few of the most destructive and deadly to strike the continental United States, Hawai'i, and Puerto Rico.

The United States started giving storms female names in 1953; by 1978, both male and female names were used for Pacific storms. The system was adopted in 1979 for Atlantic storms. Naming procedures are set by the UN's World Meteorological Organization.

AUGUST 27, 1667

Hurricane is reported by white settlers in Jamestown, Virginia.

The Deadliest Hurricanes Then and Now

SEPTEMBER 23, 1815

The Great September Gale strikes New England.

OCTOBER 29, 1867

Hurricane strikes the Virgin Islands and Puerto Rico, killing 1,000.

AUGUST 27–28, 1893

Hurricane kills up to 2,500 in South Carolina.

AUGUST 8–19, 1899

Three thousand die in an East Coast hurricane.

SEPTEMBER 8, 1900

More than 8,000 die in Galveston, Texas, hurricane and flood.

SEPTEMBER 28, 1926

A destructive hurricane devastates Miami, Florida.

SEPTEMBER 21, 1938

The surprise Great New England Hurricane kills more than 600.

Timetable of Major U.S. Hurricanes

AUGUST 25–31, 1954

Hurricane Carol strikes the East Coast, inflicting severe damage.

AUGUST 19, 1955

Hurricane Diane strikes New England.

SEPTEMBER 7–10, 1965

Hurricane Betsy causes major damage in Florida and Louisiana.

AUGUST 17, 1969

Hurricane Camille attacks coastal Mississippi and Louisiana.

JUNE 14–23, 1972

Hurricane Agnes causes floods in the mid-Atlantic.

SEPTEMBER 10–25, 1989

Hurricane Hugo hits islands in the Caribbean as well as the southeast U.S.

The Deadliest Hurricanes Then and Now

AUGUST 24, 1992

Hurricane Andrew breaks the 1989 record for damage set by Hugo.

AUGUST 29, 2005

Hurricane Katrina becomes the U.S. hurricane causing the most damage to that date.

AUGUST 24, 2017

Hurricane Harvey ties Katrina for damage, with heavy floods in Texas.

SEPTEMBER 20, 2017

Hurricane Maria strikes Puerto Rico, causing the third-most damage.

NOAA NATIONAL HURRICANE CENTER LIST OF THE COSTLIEST

NOAA satellite image of Hurricane Andrew.

This is a list of the top ten costliest tropical cyclones to strike the mainland United States. To see the full

The Deadliest Hurricanes Then and Now

list and a table with figures adjusted for inflation, visit:
https://www.nhc.noaa.gov/news/UpdatedCostliest
.pdf.

(Updated 1/26/18)

HURRICANE	YEAR	CATEGORY	DOLLARS OF DAMAGE
Katrina	2005	3	125 billion
Harvey	2017	4	125 billion
Maria	2017	4	90 billion
Sandy	2012	1	65 billion
Irma	2017	4	50 billion
Ike	2008	2	30 billion
Andrew	1992	5	27 billion
Ivan	2004	3	20.5 billion
Wilma	2005	3	19 billion
Rita	2005	3	18.5 billion

EXPLORE MORE
Internet Resources
and Lesson Plans

Education World Hurricane Lesson Plans
https://www.educationworld.com/a_lesson/lesson
/lesson076.shtml

Galveston Hurricane Slideshow
https://rosenberg-library.org/special-collections
/the-1900-storm-a-slideshow

**NEA—Activities and Lesson Plans
for K–5 Students**
http://www.nea.org/tools/lessons/hurricane-season
-grades-k-5.html

NOAA—Galveston Hurricane of 1900
https://celebrating200years.noaa.gov/magazine/galv
_hurricane/welcome.html

NOAA—National Hurricane Center
https://www.nhc.noaa.gov

NOAA—Explore Hurricanes in History
https://www.nhc.noaa.gov/outreach/history

SELECTED BIBLIOGRAPHY

Books

Beasley, Ellen. *The Alleys and Back Buildings of Galveston: An Architectural and Social History.* College Station, TX: Texas A&M University Press, 1996.

Bixel, Patricia B., and Elizabeth Hayes Turner. *Galveston and the 1900 Storm.* Austin, TX: University of Texas Press, 2008.

Cline, Joseph L. *When the Heavens Frowned.* Gretna, LA: Mathis Van Hort and Co., 1946.

Collins, Izola. *Island of Color: Where Juneteenth Started.* Bloomington, IN: AuthorHouse, 2004.

Emanuel, Kerry. *Divine Wind: The History and Science of Hurricanes.* Oxford and New York: Oxford University Press, 2005.

Greene, Casey E., and Shelly Henley Kelly, eds. *Through a Night of Horrors: Voices from the 1900 Galveston Storm.* College Station, TX: Texas A&M University Press, 2000.

Halstead, Murat. *Galveston: The Horrors of a Stricken City.* Forgotten Books, 2016. (Reproduction of 1900 book, originally published by American Publishers' Association.)

Larson, Eric. *Isaac's Storm: A Man, a Time, and the Deadliest Hurricane in History.* New York: Vintage Books, 1999.

Lester, Paul. *The Great Galveston Disaster.* Good Press, 2019. (Reproduction of 1900 book.)

McComb, David G. *Galveston: A History*. Austin, TX: University of Texas Press, 1986.

Roker, Al. *The Storm of the Century: Tragedy, Heroism, Survival, and the Epic True Story of America's Deadliest Natural Disaster: The Great Gulf Hurricane of 1900*. New York: William Morrow, 2015.

Schumacher, Michael. *November's Fury: The Deadly Great Lakes Hurricane of 1913*. Minneapolis: University of Minnesota Press, 2013.

Weems, John Edward. *A Weekend in September*. College Station, TX: Texas A&M University Press, 2002.

Articles, Newspapers, and Websites
Cline, Isaac M. *Monthly Weather Review*, Vol. 28, No. 9, September 1900, 373.

————. "West India Hurricanes," *Galveston News*, July 16, 1891.

Galveston & Texas History Center. 1900 Storm. https://www.galvestonhistorycenter.org /research/1900-storm.

Lienhard, John H. *Engines of Our Ingenuity*, Episode 865: "Raising Galveston." University of Houston College of Engineering. https://uh.edu/engines /epi865.htm.

Spillane, Richard. "The Wrecking of Galveston." *New York Times*, September 11, 1900.

SOURCE NOTES

Source notes tell us where a quotation came from, such as an oral history, interview, newspaper article, or book. In nonfiction, facts and research are important, so authors also use source notes to let readers know where they have obtained specific facts or details. The notes here are organized by chapters. Paying attention to source notes helps us become better readers, researchers, and writers too.

Prologue
"I saw a roof . . .": Harry I. Maxson in Greene and Kelly, *Through a Night of Horrors*, 129.

Before You Begin
"I remember passing . . .": Collins, *Island of Color*, 7.

About the People in This Book
Mary Louise Bristol (Hopkins): Hopkins obituary, *Galveston Daily News*, November 21, 1987, https://www.newspapers.com/image/?clipping_id=19318369&fcfToken=eyJhbGciOiJIUzI1NiIsIn

R5cCI6IkpXVCJ9.eyJmcmVlLXZpZXXctaWQiOjExNTA4MTcyL-CJpYXQiOjE1ODEwMjk3MzcsImV4cCI6MTU4MTExNjEzN30.VUp_MmrvKtmLQnLOXv7hFXg7Nv0sVSq8K8rrkHnXjt0.

Milton Elford: Find a Grave, https://www.findagrave.com/memorial/48421992/john-elford.

Katherine Vedder (Pauls): Find a Grave, https://www.findagrave.com/memorial/71991068/katharine-pauls.

Arnold R. Wolfram: Find a Grave, https://www.findagrave.com/memorial/87069814/arnold-rudolph-wolfram.

Chapter 1
"The hurricane which visited . . .": I. M. Cline, "Monthly Weather Review."

"It was a perfect . . .": Katherine Vedder Pauls in Greene and Kelly, 180.

Galveston in 1900: Greene and Kelly, 3.

Cline address: Larson, *Isaac's Storm*, 7.

"the only area . . .": Collins, 17–18.

Hurricane formation: https://spaceplace.nasa.gov/hurricanes/en/.

heights of ten or eleven feet: Emanuel, *Divine Wind*, 7.

the word *hurricane*: Ibid., 18.

Chapter 2
Brazos River: Roker, 79.

Elevation: Lienhard, "Raising Galveston."

"It would be impossible . . .": I. M. Cline, "West India Hurricanes."

Cuba weather observers: Roker, 89–93.

"'We are today . . .'": Larson, 111.

"If Gangoite's prediction . . .": Ibid., 96.

Source Notes

"The usual signs . . .": I. M. Cline, "Monthly Weather Review."

Storm Definitions: https://phys.org/news/2015-03-cyclone-hurricane
-typhoon-violent-phenomenon.html.; Emanuel, 18–21.

Chapter 3

"On the dark, cold winter . . .": J. L. Cline, *When the Heavens Frowned*, 1.

"I applied myself . . .": Ibid., 34.

Swells: Ibid., 133.

"Unusually heavy swells . . .": I. M. Cline, "Monthly Weather Review."

"'The weather bureau . . .'": Larson, 143.

"Friday evening . . .": Sarah Hawley in Greene and Kelly, 28.

"Gulf rising . . .": I. M. Cline, "Monthly Weather Review."

"indicate the great intensity . . .": Ibid.

Torricelli: http://chemed.chem.purdue.edu/genchem/history/torricelli
.html.

lowest barometer: https://www.guinnessworldrecords.com/world-records
/lowest-barometric-pressure?fb_comment_id=724903447587744_1561
623120582435.

Chapter 4

"The wreck of Galveston . . .": Spillane, "Wrecking of Galveston."

Cline house: Larson, 7.

"like a lighthouse . . .": J. L. Cline, 52.

"At this time . . .": I. M. Cline, "Monthly Weather Review."

"The water rose . . .": Ibid.

Winds: Emanuel, 88.

Chapter 5

"About half past three . . .": Katherine Vedder Pauls in Greene and Kelly, 180.

"The house rose . . .": Ibid., 181.

Galveston in 1900: Greene and Kelly, 3.

"handed us . . .": Katherine Vedder Pauls in Greene and Kelly, 181.

"I called out . . .": Ibid.

"But for months . . .": Ibid., 182.

"My mother took him . . .": Ibid.

"Gradually the tiny body . . .": Ibid.

"all it takes . . .": https://www.noaa.gov/stories/tropical-storms-and-hurricanes-in-winter-and-spring.

Chapter 6

"It was as if . . .": Harry I. Maxson in Greene and Kelly, 130.

"I returned home . . .": Ibid., 130–31.

"Father anticipated . . .": Ibid., 131.

"We had no tools . . .": Ibid.

"I heard what I didn't . . .": Ibid., 132.

"I thanked him . . .": Ibid., 133.

Chapter 7

"near level . . .": Collins, 279.

"When I got . . .": Ibid., 279–80.

"When we [hit] . . .": Ibid., 280.

"Just did get away!": Ibid., 281.

"About 5 [o'clock] it grew worse . . .": Milton Elford in Halstead, Galveston, 212.

Source Notes

"All at once . . .": Ibid., 212–13.

"I had only got . . .": Ibid., 213.

"I was hit on the head . . .": Ibid.

"We must have all gone . . .": Ibid.

"The street was full . . .": Ibid.

"At the corner . . .": Arnold Wolfram in Greene and Kelly, 119.

"I shouted to him . . .": Ibid.

"We were now forcing . . .": Ibid., 120.

"We were both suddenly . . .": Ibid., 121.

"The air was full . . .": Ibid.

"I remember seeing . . .": Mary Louise Bristol Hopkins in Greene and Kelly, 170.

"She got an axe . . .": Ibid., 171.

"She realized that the house . . .": Ibid.

"My mother would say . . .": Ibid., 172.

Chapter 8
"I urged them . . .": J. L. Cline, 53–54.

"I seized the hand . . .": Ibid., 54.

"It was raining in torrents . . .": Ibid.

"We remained close together . . .": Ibid., 56.

"I made a lunge for him . . .": Ibid., 57.

"Tired and unspeakably battered . . .": Ibid., 59.

Chapter 9
Death toll: https://www.galvestonhistorycenter.org/research/1900-storm.

"'Papa, where are . . .'": Ibid.

"Not a plank . . .": Ibid.

"No streets or roads . . .": Ibid.

"'You know, my grandmother . . .'": Ibid., 185.

"I turned away . . .": Arnold Wolfram in Greene and Kelly, 122.

"I dreaded to look . . .": Ibid.

"The little lad . . .": Ibid., 123.

"She told me . . .": Collins, 272–73.

Henry Johnson: Beasley, *Alleys and Back Buildings*, 69.

"These white people . . .": Collins, 281.

"As soon as it was light . . .": Halstead, 214.

"It seems that I have . . .": Ibid., 211.

"There are hundreds . . .": Ibid., 212.

"I have been helping . . .": Ibid., 211.

"The law would come . . .": Collins, 282.

"It is the most awful . . .": Halstead, 214–15.

"Hundreds of families . . .": Ibid., 215.

"It was all over . . .": Ibid.

"They were told . . .": Mary Louise Bristol Hopkins in Greene and Kelly, 172–73.

"We went to the back porch . . .": Ibid.

"What a wreck it left . . .": Harry I. Maxson in Greene and Kelly, 134.

"About 35th and Avenue P . . .": Ibid., 135.

"I tried to get him . . .": Ibid., 136.

"Many of my friends . . .": Ibid., 139.

Source Notes

Chapter 10

"Not a house was left . . .": J. L. Cline, 60.

"Acting upon a sudden . . .": Ibid., 61.

"Many years later . . .": Ibid., 62.

Cora Goldbeck: https://ancestors.familysearch.org/en/L7B1-KC1/cora-audrey-goldbeck-1892-1987.

"But we investigated . . .": Thomas Monagan in Greene and Kelly, 103.

"So they had brought . . .": Ibid.

"We walked over . . .": Ibid., 104.

Donations: Larson, 244–45.

"'To the Lodges . . .'": Lester, *The Great Galveston Disaster*, 261.

"'Contracts were made . . .'": Beasley, 70.

"night of horror.": J. L. Cline, 134.

Epilogue

NOAA: https://www.nhc.noaa.gov/news/UpdatedCostliest.pdf.

Deadly cyclones: Emanuel, 263–64.

PHOTO CREDITS

Photos ©: cover: James P Reed/Corbis via Getty Images, Joe Raedle/Getty Images; Kenneth K. Lam/ Baltimore Sun/Tribune News Service via Getty Images, Mario Tama/Getty Images, Samuel Maciel/ iStock/Getty Images, Scott Olson/Getty Images, AFP via Getty Images, Warren Faidley/The Image Bank/ Getty Images, all other photos: Shutterstock.com; i: NOAA; iv–v, x: Library of Congress; xi: Courtesy of Peter Flagg Maxson; xxiv–1, 139: NOAA National Environmental Satellite, Data, and Information Service (NESDIS); 12: NOAA/JPL-Caltech; 14, 16, 20–21, 28, 32, 38–39: NOAA; 45: U.S. Navy/NOAA; 47: Library of Congress; 50: National Archives (27-S-23b-305); 60, 65, 68: Library of Congress; 72: NOAA; 83: Library of Congress; 86–87: Associated Press/AP

Images; 96–97: National Archives (27-S-23b-306); 99, 107, 120: Library of Congress; 123: NOAA; 124: Debbie Larson/NWS/NOAA; 126: NOAA; 128: Barbara Ambrose/NODC/NCDDC/NOAA; 129, 131: Carol M. Highsmith's America, Library of Congress; 159: NOAA; 181: NOAA National Environmental Satellite, Data, and Information Service (NESDIS).

INDEX

Page numbers in *italics* refer to illustrations.

Atlantic (Ocean/Coast) 11, 14, 19, 24–25, 27, 53, 78, 125, 135, 142, 147, 155, 157

atmosphere 4, 36, 54, 135, 141–43

barometers 21, 35–37, 141, 148, 151

Barton, Clara xix, 116–17

Blagdon, John D. 17, 35

Bristol, Mary Louise xix, 75–77, 104–05, 118

Caribbean 15, 19, 22, 125, 157

climate change/global warming 47, 134–36, 146

climatologists 134–36

Cline, Cora 4, 6, 42, 82, 84–85, 112

Cline, Isaac xx, 3–4, 6, 17–20, 24, 30–35, 41–43, *45*, 46, 62, 80–85, *83*, 112–113, 122

Cline, Joseph xx, 17, 30–31,

34, 41–43, 80–85, 113–14, 122

Collins, Izola xv, xvi, xxi–ii, 9–10, 66, 95, 98

Cuba 22–23, 25, 122

Cuney, Norris Wright 8

cyclones 18, 27, 29, 54, 125, 136, 141–42, 146–47, 155, 159

Dent, Jessie 9, 10

Elford, Milton xxi, 66–67, *68*, 100–01, 103

Emergency Supplies Checklist 110–11

eyewall 13, *38*, 141, 148, 150

FEMA 111, 116

Florida 14, 22, *32*, 125, 127, 156–57

Galveston
city xv, 3–4, 5–10, 115, 121

Galveston (*cont.*)

 Great Hurricane *iv–v*, vi, *x*,
  xi, xiii, xv–xvi, xix–xxiii,
  1, 3–4, 14, 17–18, 20,
  20–21, 24–25, 33–34, 39,
  41, 44–45, *45*, 47, *50*, 53,
  60, 62, 70, 78, 83, *86*, 92,
  95, *96–97*, 98, 101–02,
  105, 109–10, 113, 115,
  117–19, *120*, 121–22, 125,
  127, 131–32, 137–38, 156,
  161–62

 hurricane victims *96–97*,
  98, 106, *120*, 137–38

 Island 17, 42, 46, 83, 92,
  115–16,

 segregation and racial
  prejudice in 7–8, 10, 98

 survivors xv, 82, 85, *86*,
  89–109, 114, 117, 122

Gangoite, Fr. Lorenzo 23–25,
 122

Geostationary satellite
 (GOES) 15, 142, 146

Goldbeck, Cora 113–14

greenhouse effect 135, 142

Gulf of Mexico xii–xiii, 5–6,
 14, 17–18, 20, 24–25, 31,
 34, 42, 46, 75, 83, 85, *97*,
 112, 121, 127

Havana, Cuba 22–24

Hurácan 15

hurricane formation 12–16

Hurricane Hunters 16

Hurricane Andrew 158, *159*,
 160

Hurricane Camille 157

Hurricane Caroline 16

Hurricane Frederic *123*

Hurricane Harvey 78, 130,
 132, 136, 158, 160

Hurricane Hugo 157–58

Hurricane Irma 160

Hurricane Ivan 160

Hurricane Katrina 78, 126,
 126, 127–31, *128*, *129*,
 131, 152, 160

Hurricane Maria *xxiv*, 78,
 132–33, 158, 160

Hurricane Mitch*124*

Hurricane Rita 78, 160

Hurricane Wilma 78, 160

hurricanes, categories of
 61–62, 144, 149, 160

hurricanes, list of the costliest
 159–60

Jover, Julio 23–24

Juneteenth xv, 7

Lake Borgne 128

Lake Pontchartrain 128

Lee, Opal 7

Louisiana 14, 127, 130,
 157

Index

Maxson, Harry *x*, , xi, *xi*, xxi, 55–60, 76, 105–06, 108–09

McCullough, Annie Smizer xvi, xxi–xxii, 63–66, *65*, 95, 98, 102

McGuire, Robert 9, 10

meteorologists 23, 27, 134

meteorology 4, 31, 143, 148

Miami *126*, 156

Mississippi 14, 127, *128*, *131*, 157

Monagan, Thomas xxii, 115–16

Moore, Willis 19, 22–23, 25–26, 122

National Hurricane Center 53, 62, 78–79, 152, 160, 162

New Orleans xx, 24, 122, 127–29, *129*

NOAA *xxiv*,*12*, 14–16, *14*, 19, *38*, 44, 53–54, 62, 78–79, 132, 134, 136, 142–44, 151–52, 159, 162

Pacific Ocean 27–28, 142, 146–47, 155

Puerto Rico *xxiv*, 127, 132–33, 155–56, 158

radar 15, 19, *123*, *126*, 143

Roker, Al 24

Saffir-Simpson Hurricane Wind Scale 61, 144

Sahara Desert 11

Scull, Horace 6–9

Scull, Ralph Albert xvi, xxii, 6, 9, 95

seawall 18, 121, 138, 145

Stockman, William 22–23

storm surges xii, *32*, 42, 44–45, *45*, 80, 121, 128, 135, 137, 145, 147–8

Texas vi, xi, 1, 3, 5, 7, 10, 14, 18, 20, 24, 25, 75, 98, 113–14, 118–19, 122, 132, 136–37, 156, 158

Timetable of Major U.S. Hurricanes 155–58

Torricelli, Evangelista 36

tropics 11, 145

tsunami 150

typhoon 27, 37, 146, 147–8, 150

Unscramble 149

U.S. Weather Bureau 3, 19, 22, 25, 32, 33, 122

forecasters *xxiv*, 16, 18, 21, 23–25, 29, 36, 134, 151

observers xx, 4, 15, 17, 19, 21, 22, 30

satellites *xxiv*, 15, 18 134, 142, 146, 150, *159*

Vedder, Katherine xxiii, 3, 46–52, *47, 50*, 57, 89–92
Viñes, Fr. Benito 23

Washington, DC 7, 19, 22, 32, 33, 34
Wolfram, Arnold R. xxiii, 70–74, *72*, 93–94

One of the deadliest hurricanes in modern times was Hurricane Katrina. This NOAA satellite image of Katrina was taken on August 28, 2005, when the storm was at its peak intensity.

ABOUT THE AUTHOR

Deborah Hopkinson is an award-winning author of picture books, middle grade fiction, and nonfiction. Her nonfiction titles include *We Must Not Forget: Holocaust Stories of Survival and Resistance*; *We Had to Be Brave: Escaping the Nazis on the Kindertransport*; *Titanic: Voices from the Disaster*, a Sibert Medal Honor Book and YALSA Award for Excellence in Nonfiction finalist; *Courage & Defiance: Stories of Spies, Saboteurs, and Survivors in World War II Denmark*, a Sydney Taylor Notable Book, NCTE Orbis Pictus Recommended Book, and a winner of the Oregon Book Award and Oregon Spirit Award; *Dive! World War II Stories of Sailors & Submarines in the Pacific*, an NCTE Orbis Pictus Recommended Book and Oregon Spirit Award

Honor Book; and *D-Day: The World War II Invasion That Changed History.*

Deborah lives with her family near Portland, Oregon, along with an assortment of pets that includes two canine office companions (Brooklyn and Rue); one cat (Beatrix); three chickens (Daisy, Chuckles, and Georgina); canaries named for #GOT characters; and an assortment of finches and fish. When she's not traveling the country to talk about history with students, Deborah is at the gym or attempting to create a garden. She also reads a lot. Visit her online at www.deborahhopkinson.com and follow her on Twitter at @Deborahopkinson and on Instagram at @deborah_hopkinson.